HUGH O'FLAHERTY
HIS WARTIME ADVENTURES

ALISON WALSH

D1364022

The Collins Press

First published in 2010 by
The Collins Press
West Link Park
Doughcloyne
Wilton
Cork

© Alison Walsh 2010

Alison Walsh has asserted her moral right to be identified as the author of this work.

A Cataloguing in Publication data record for this book is available from the British Library.

ISBN: 978-184889-058-9

Typesetting by The Collins Press
Typeset in Bembo
Printed in Great Britain by CPI Cox & Wyman

This book is based on Brian Fleming's *The Vatican Pimpernel*.

To Eoin, Niamh and Cian

Contents

Cast of Characters

Hugh O'Flaherty, Monsignor, founder of the Rome Escape Organisation.

John May, his fixer and helper, one of the Council of Three.

Major Sam Derry, Hugh's trusted second-in-command in the organisation, one of the Council of Three in charge of administration.

Count Sarsfield Salazar, final member of the Council of Three, a member of the Swiss Legation.

The organisation's helpers:

Delia Murphy, popular singer and wife to the Irish Minister, Thomas Kiernan.

Molly Stanley, a British woman living in Rome.

Father John 'Spike' Buckley and Father Kenneth Madden, two Irish priests who became active members of the organisation, delivering medicine and goods to POWs.

Henrietta Chevalier, a Maltese widow, who sheltered many POWs, and her friend, Father Borg.

Father Owen Sneddon, a New Zealand priest.

Father Anselmo Musters, a Dutch priest.

Cast of Characters

Renzo and Adrienne Lucidi, Romans who sheltered many POWs in their home.

Iride and Maria Imperioli. Two of the organisation's key helpers near Sulmona, the POW camp south of Rome.

Prince Doria Pamphilj. Supplied the organisation with large sums of money to purchase food.

Joe Pollak, a Czech POW; Lieutenant Bill Simpson; Lieutenant John Furman. Escaped from Chieti POW camp and became key members of the organisation, in charge of delivering supplies and guiding escapees to their accommodation.

Flight Lieutenant Garrad-Cole, an escaped British POW.

Mother Mary St Luke, an American nun living in Rome, who kept a detailed diary of daily life in the city during the War. She would later publish this diary under a pen name, Jane Scrivener. Dr Thomas Kiernan, Irish Minister to the Holy See.

Sir D'Arcy Osborne, British Minister to the Holy See.

Harold H. Tittman, United States Representative to the Holy See.

Ernst von Weizsaecker, German Ambassador to the Holy See.

Lieutenant Colonel Herbert Kappler, Head of the Gestapo in Rome.

Pietro Caruso, Fascist Chief of Police.

Pietro Koch, Chief of the Fascist police squad.

The Vatican.

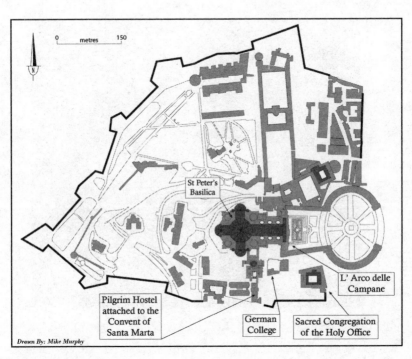

Map of the Vatican.

Prologue
A Dangerous Situation

Unaware that he was being watched, Monsignor Hugh O'Flaherty sat chatting with his friend, Prince Doria, on an autumn day in 1943. They were in an upstairs room of the Prince's Palazzo, a very grand house on Via del Corso in Rome. The Prince was a generous supporter of the cause, and wanted to give the Monsignor money to buy supplies for those he was helping to escape. The Second World War had by now been raging for four years and the city was full of escaped prisoners of war, and Hugh had made it his mission to help them.

The Prince's secretary waited a discreet distance from the two friends, looking out on to the pavement below. He noticed a sudden commotion outside on the street: a large force of grey-uniformed Gestapo officers was on the move. With horror, the Prince's secretary realised they were heading straight for the Palazzo.

'Quick,' he cried, 'Kappler's men are coming.'

The three men were aghast. The Gestapo must have followed Hugh to the Palazzo and now they were coming to capture him.

'Run,' said Prince Doria, 'we'll delay them as long as we can.'

'Thank you, my boy,' said the Monsignor as he leapt to his feet and hurried out.

The Palazzo was a maze of rooms and the Monsignor found his way down to the basement, clutching the Prince's money in his hand. Upstairs, his friends tried to keep the Gestapo out for as long as possible. Frantically, O'Flaherty searched the basement for an escape route. If the Gestapo captured him, he would certainly be imprisoned, or worse, put to death.

His fear was not just for himself, though, but also for his friends: they would be executed by the Germans if they were found helping a wanted man. And Hugh was Rome's most wanted man at that time. Lieutenant Colonel Herbert Kappler, head of the Gestapo in the Italian city, had ordered that the Monsignor be captured or killed.

Upstairs, the door crashed open and the Gestapo poured in . . . Hugh was trapped.

1 Learning the Ropes

Hugh O'Flaherty's extraordinary life began in an ordinary way. He was born in 1898 in Kerry and grew up with his sister and two brothers in the lodge at Killarney Golf Club, where his father was caretaker.

He was a happy, gentle boy who loved sport. He was an expert golfer and enjoyed handball, hurling, boxing and swimming. But he was also a strong student, who wanted nothing more than to become a priest. It was clear that Hugh possessed many qualities for this role: he was compassionate, brave and able to see the best in everyone. And even though they weren't wealthy, his parents were delighted to have a student priest in the family. 'I would sell the house to make a priest of him,' his father declared.

In 1918, when Hugh went to Mungret College in Limerick to continue his training, it was a turbulent time in Ireland. British forces still occupied the country and many citizens were being shot and killed. In fact, Hugh was arrested coming back from a visit to the home of one victim in Limerick and only released at the request of the Rector of Mungret College.

When he was sent to Rome to complete his studies, in 1922, he would find that it was a beautiful place, just like Ireland, but not a peaceful one. The Fascist dictator, Benito Mussolini, had just come to power. 'Il Duce' as he was called, banned all other political parties, took away the rights of ordinary Italians and imposed a rule that was total. Every day, a new law would be made, and the people lived in terror.

But Hugh was initially more concerned with his academic studies in theology and philosophy that would qualify him to become a priest. The studies were hard and demanded a lot of the young Hugh. He wrote to his sister Bride that, 'I just fluked through and no more . . . I went in for the exam in the evening with a cold perspiration all over . . . because five went in that morning and only one got through the ordeal with success!'

But he did succeed and in July, he wrote to Bride again, 'but there are also three letters before Hugh. "Rev" after July 12th. It was a great day.'

Others were quick to spot the talent in this young Irishman, notably his mentor, Monsignor Dini. Within three years, Hugh had been promoted to the rank of Monsignor and some years later, was called away to do important diplomatic work for the Church in

The O'Flaherty family in the mid-1920s (left to right): Hugh, his sister Bride, his parents, Margaret and James, and his two brothers, Jim and Neil.

Czechoslovakia for two years. And even though he never said what he had been doing there, it was clear that it was a very sensitive mission which had taught him many lessons.

When Hugh returned to the Eternal City, he found a place in turmoil. Mussolini had the city in a vice-like grip, issuing law after law. Hugh wrote to Bride's husband, Chris, a shopkeeper: 'Yesterday, they published a list of shopkeepers who were selling inferior goods . . . they must now close. Besides the latest law makes people walk in [to shops] on the right-hand side . . . added to this we have the unmarried tax and a tax for the married who have no children. Il Duce is doing well.'

Although Hugh's letter tried to make light of the situation for his sister and her family, living in Rome was becoming more difficult by the day. Whilst Mussolini might have improved transport and given many Italians jobs, he ruled the city and the country with an iron fist. All teachers had to swear an oath of allegiance to the Fascist Party; all newspaper editors had to be personally approved by him. Then, as the Second World War loomed, Mussolini joined forces with Hitler and in summer 1941 Italy joined the War on the German side.

Italy and Rome were thrown into turmoil. Many prisoners of war, or POWs, were in camps throughout the north of Italy. Other Italians went into hiding to avoid being drafted into the army. And many people in Rome, too, would find their lives in danger.

At the beginning of the War, Hugh listened to the propaganda of both sides in the conflict, the Allies who had stood up to Hitler when he had invaded another country, and their enemies, the Germans and the Italians. He wasn't sure what to believe. After all, he had seen at first hand how the British had ruled his country and how many Irish people had suffered. But then, in 1942, he saw a photograph in the newspaper *Il Messaggero*. Fifty Jews had been rounded up and forced to scrub the roads along the Tiber, old men and respectable ladies on their hands and knees, a sight which horrified O'Flaherty. Even though Mussolini forbade Jews from studying or teaching in any Italian school or university, and removed all books written by Jews from libraries, they were permitted to stay in the country. However, when the Germans seized direct power in 1943 after the fall of Mussolini, they were determined to target the Jews in Rome and to exterminate them. These horrors would make their mark on Hugh O'Flaherty, as he confided to his great friend, Sam Derry: 'they treated them like beasts . . . you know the sort of thing that happened after that; it got worse and worse and I knew then which side I had to believe.'

2 A New Vocation

The photograph in *Il Messaggero* was a turning point for Hugh. He knew that it was no longer enough for him to say prayers and Mass to help the people of Rome. He needed to act. 'Everybody knows Monsignor O'Flaherty and, what's more, they all adore him,' one of his closest colleagues said. Hugh had made many friends during his time in Rome, and decided to make use of his contacts in the city to help those who needed it most.

In this, Hugh knew that the Vatican itself would play a vital role. His home and his refuge, it was also an independent city-state. This meant that even though it was in the middle of Rome, it was, in fact, a little country with its own government and its own laws, not those of Mussolini. Anyone who needed refuge would find it there, safe from the Fascists. But its position was on a knife-edge. The Vatican knew that the Fascists could easily change their minds . . .

Knowing that their every move was being watched, the Vatican police, called the Swiss Guards, were ordered to turn away those seeking refuge. But the Fascists had their spies in the Vatican among the many servants who worked there and even placed agents in churches, where they knew people would approach priests for help. Hugh knew that he had to be careful.

One day, a group of fourteen men gathered in St Peter's Square. Their clothes were shabby and worn, and they looked hungry and worried. It was clear that they had not come to hear Mass or to admire St Peter's, but were escaped POWs, looking to find shelter. Hugh did not want to disobey his orders and so he asked a friend, Antonio Call, a policeman who hated the Fascists, to help. The men were smuggled into the Vatican, two at a time. But the very next day, they were expelled. Thankfully, O'Flaherty had many friends, sometimes in unexpected places. The fourteen men would find themselves being fed and looked after in a police barracks for the next year, until the Germans marched into Rome.

Hugh helped many more people to escape from the Fascists, finding them places to stay, giving them food and money, often hiding them in his own home. And even though his life was in danger many times, this brave priest would save 6,500 lives by the time the War was over.

As the War took hold, Mussolini's grip on power loosened. There were grumblings in the army that he was not a strong enough leader. Some even suggested mounting a *coup d'état*, in which the army would take over government. Many wanted Italy to withdraw from the War altogether, but Mussolini thought it just too soon. Victory was still possible, he thought, even though the Allied forces were approaching Sicily, to liberate the country. On 10 July, they invaded.

Less than a month earlier, Il Duce had sworn that any enemy soldier setting foot on Italian soil would not live to tell the tale. He had clearly been mistaken. Worse, he looked weak. On 25 July, he was dismissed by the King. People rushed into the streets to celebrate. They shouted 'Long live the King! Long live free Italy!' and 'Down with Mussolini!'

But their joy was to be short-lived. The Germans, wanting to make sure that Italy remained in their hands, marched on Rome.

3 A Clerical Coalman

Henrietta Chevalier was a widow and mother to eight children, who lived in a small third-floor apartment on Via dell'Impero. One day, her son, Paul, rang the apartment and said, 'Tell Mama that I am bringing home two books.' Unsure what he meant, Henrietta waited, and later that afternoon he appeared, not with two books under his arm, but with two strange men.

Paul had taken no chances on the telephone. Rome was in the grip of the Germans, who had marched on the city in 1943, after the fall of the dictator Mussolini. The Romans, who had celebrated his departure with bonfires and parties on the streets, now lived in fear of their new rulers, who imposed a regime of terror. No one was allowed to write letters, the Germans listened in to phone calls and watched their every move. And with the Gestapo in charge of security in the city, if anyone was found helping POWs to escape, the consequences would surely be deadly.

Henrietta Chevalier, the brave Maltese widow who played a huge role in Hugh O'Flaherty's organisation.

John May, 'scrounger' and helper of the Rome Escape Organisation.

Who were these strangers, Henrietta wondered. Her son explained that they were French POWs and that Monsignor O'Flaherty would be visiting her later that evening, with a very special request. Without hesitating, Henrietta agreed to shelter the POWs and many others that Hugh brought to her. Even though her flat was tiny and only had two bedrooms, sometimes she had as many as nine guests lying on mattresses on the dining-room floor. She looked after them well, cooking and cleaning and sending her daughters out into the city in search of food. And Hugh used his network of Roman friends to make false papers for the men, so that they could roam the city freely.

But Hugh could not act alone: he relied on a network of friends in this city to help him do his work. One of his great allies at this time was John May, the manservant of the British Minister to the Holy See, D'Arcy Osborne.

Aware that the Germans were watching his every move, Osborne knew that he could not help directly, but instead offered the services of John. A clever man, he was able to find anything and wasn't afraid to use the black market to get what he needed, or even to bribe people. Hugh was so taken with him he called him, 'Indispensable, a genius, the most significant scrounger I have ever come across.' May, along with the Swiss Ambassador, Count Sarsfield Salazar, was O'Flaherty's staunch ally during this time. Salazar's job was to get food and money to those POWs hiding in the countryside around Rome.

Aware that people as brave as Henrietta were scarce, Hugh rented a flat on Via Firenze to hide other POWs, amused that it faced Gestapo headquarters. 'Faith,' he chortled, 'they'll not look under their noses!'

Keeping these two apartments running and feeding and clothing the 'guests' required a lot of money. And so, Hugh turned to another friend, Prince Doria Pamphilj, who gave him the princely sum of £2,000. Of course, this money could not be given openly and a network of people carried it through the streets of Rome. Some of them were not even aware of what they were carrying: one young nun, Noreen Dennehy, was surprised when Monsignor O'Flaherty asked her to bring a letter to a princess, and to return with the reply. Why is it that he could not go down and pick it up himself, she wondered. After all, he had a car. Only after the War was she told what she had been carrying, with the words, 'you were very lucky that you weren't held up or put in jail'.

It was only a matter of time, though, before the Gestapo learned what Hugh was doing. As well as friends and allies, Rome was full of spies and informers. Kappler, the head of the Gestapo in Rome, had been keeping a very close eye on the Monsignor and his friends. And, one evening, when O'Flaherty visited Prince Doria in his Palazzo on Via del Corso, they pounced.

With only moments to spare before Kappler and his Gestapo officers swarmed through the building, Hugh ran down to the basement of the Palazzo, a maze of underground rooms. Determined not to panic, he searched until he noticed a patch of light filtering through a hatch in the basement. It was a coal cellar. He scrambled up the small pile of coal and looked out of the hatch on to the street. He was in luck: the coalmen were delivering to the Palazzo. There, in front of him, were two coalmen, looking at the twenty Gestapo officers gathered at the door of the Palazzo, about to gain entry.

O'Flaherty grabbed one of the coal-sacks which had been lying on the ground and pulled it gently through the hatch. Then he removed his heavy clothes – his long black coat with its rows of buttons, and his shirt, leaving only his vest and trousers on. He then smeared coal dust on himself. His disguise was complete.

'Get on with it,' one of the Gestapo yelled at the coalman, who hurried towards the hatch, to find himself face to face with Monsignor O'Flaherty, covered in coal dust, with his priest's clothes in a coal sack on his back. Somehow, Hugh managed to persuade the frightened man that he was really a priest and to his relief, the man believed him, clambering in the coal hatch to help the Monsignor.

Moments later, a tall man, covered in coal dust, clambered out of the hatch onto the street. As far as the

Gestapo were aware, the coalman had made his delivery. Calmly, the man walked towards the lorry, and then vanished out of sight.

A short while later, the sacristan of a local church was startled by the sudden appearance of a man with a black face and dirty clothes, saying that he was a priest. The sacristan decided to believe him and allowed him to clean up and change back into his clothes. Within moments, the Monsignor had vanished again through the back streets of the city.

Some hours later, Prince Doria's phone rang. 'I am back home now, are you well my boy?' the Monsignor's voice was soft.

'Fine now,' the Prince said. 'Some day you must tell me how you did it. I'm afraid Colonel Kappler is a very angry man. He spent two hours here and he did say that if I happened to see you, that one of these days, he will be entertaining you . . .'

Even though John May had provided Hugh with a number of disguises – including that of a nun – after his narrow escape from Prince Doria's Palazzo, he knew that he had to stop roaming the streets for a while. At six feet two inches tall and with his distinctive mop of dark hair and glasses, he was easily recognisable. Instead, he would wait at the steps of St Peter's Basilica, saying his prayers and waiting for those who needed help to approach him.

And there were many. One evening, a friend of the Monsignor's, an Irish woman called Molly Stanley, came to visit him. She had worrying news about his old friend, Prince Doria. He had been betrayed to Kappler, the head of the Gestapo in Rome, and had one hour to escape. Thinking on his feet, Hugh asked John May to find a Swiss Guard's uniform and sent another priest off to get the Prince, urging him to hurry, that time was of the essence. Dashing through the streets, the Prince was brought to St Monica's monastery where he changed into the uniform. Once darkness fell, Hugh and the Prince went to hide in the shadows of the Bernini Colonnade, the vast stone pillars which led to St Peter's. They waited as quietly as they could until the stroke of midnight, when the Swiss Guard changed. When the soldiers passed, they didn't notice the new soldier who melted into their company, marching alongside them into the square. And then he was gone . . .

Hugh would face many challenges in his work, but none more satisfying than the help he gave to a fellow countryman, an Irish Guards officer called Colin Lesslie. Lesslie had been captured in Tunisia and moved to Italy for medical treatment, but as soon as he got the chance, he escaped. Knowing that his best chance of safety lay in Rome, Lesslie made his way to the Apennine Mountains, the rugged range which stretches all the way down the country, the 'backbone' of Italy. Desperate for food and shelter, he persuaded a local shepherd to take him in. Of course, the peasant risked death if Lesslie was discovered in his home, and as winter drew in, the officer knew that he needed to move on.

A lucky fluke provided him with food and enough money for his train fare to Rome, where he knew that he would find shelter, as long as he aimed for the Vatican. He got onto the train bound for Rome, and took his seat – next to five officers of the SS, Hitler's most feared soldiers, with their sinister black uniforms. But the soldiers took no notice of this shabbily dressed man; after all, it was the Italians who were looking for Lesslie, not the Germans.

A chilly October wind was blowing when Lesslie got to Rome. He headed for the nearest church, knowing that his best chance of refuge lay there. After moving from church to church as the day wore on, a message was sent to Hugh that his help was needed. Under cover of darkness, Hugh set out across the city, carrying with him the uniform of a Monsignor, a long purple-trimmed cassock and small black hat called a biretta. And even though Lesslie was very tall, as he and Hugh marched into the Vatican, he looked every inch an important cleric.

Lesslie was safe at last, but he had one great worry. When he was captured by the Italians, his wife, Eileen, was told that he was dead. He had to get word to her in England that he was safe. John May had an idea. Lesslie was to write a 'cheque' to Eileen for £5, but on a plain piece of paper, to which John stuck a stamp. This cheque found its way into the diplomatic bag, the bag which contained all the post from the Vatican and which could not be searched by the Germans. A few days later, Eileen received a phone call from her bank manager in England. Could she come to cash a cheque for £5 which had arrived that morning? Puzzled, Eileen complied. As soon as she saw the cheque, she knew: it was her husband's handwriting. He was alive.

Major Sam Derry.

4 The Honourable Englishman

As 1943 wore on, the Germans tightened their grip on Rome. In particular, they targeted the city's Jews. Even though they had been persecuted by Mussolini, they had at least been safe in the city, but now, they faced the prospect of being deported. Many people knew what this really meant: that the Jews would be taken away from the city, to Germany and the concentration camps.

But at the time, even the Roman Jews themselves were reluctant to believe this. They had not suffered in the same way as their brethren had in Germany or France, after all. And so they did not heed the warnings given by friends. On 16 October, before sunrise, the SS took action, rounding up more than a thousand Jews. Two days later, they were sent to concentration camps in Germany. Mother Mary St Luke, an American nun living in the city, observed the events of that day: 'The SS are doing exactly what one expected and at 4.30 am today, began to round up the Jews in their own houses. The Rabbi did not destroy his registers [details of the names and addresses of all Jews in his care] and they know where every Jew lives . . . it is a nameless horror.'

With the persecution of the Jews, food shortages and the fear instilled in the Romans by the SS, Hugh knew that the work of his organisation was more vital than ever. At the same time, there was more work than he could possibly do, even with the help of John May. The organisation needed a structure. And just as the idea took hold in Hugh's mind, a man called Sam Derry appeared.

Sam Derry was a genius at escape. In 1942, he had been captured in North Africa and escaped. The following July, he was captured again, by the very same German unit, and found his way to Chieti POW camp. There, he was one of the youngest members of the escape committee, helping to build no fewer than six tunnels out of the camp. Whenever one was discovered, another was started.

Then he was moved to Sulmona camp, but he knew that he was on his way to Germany. Very soon, he and some of his friends were ordered to march to the nearest train station, where they were pushed aboard a train and sent through northern Italy. As the train rattled through the countryside, Sam made a decision. He knew it was now or never – and so, on the spur of the moment, he jumped. He knew the risks – death, serious injury or being shot by the guards if they saw him – but the alternative was worse.

An elderly peasant couple were surprised to open their door to an oddly dressed man, who spoke no Italian. They spoke no English, but it became clear to them that this stranger needed help. After all, there were many others hiding out in this part of the country. Sam had managed to find his way to this isolated farm after jumping from the train. As night fell, two local boys led Sam to some caves, where he was astonished to see a crowd of escaped POWs, just like him. The local people were looking after them as best they could, but Sam knew that they could not survive a winter in the caves. They needed real help.

They were not far from Rome, but the enemy was everywhere and Sam did not know whom to trust. The local priest was friendly, and offered to send a message to the Vatican, which Sam knew was his only hope. And when the priest insisted that Sam meet his boss, Sam had no real choice but to agree. And so, early one November morning, Sam found himself sitting on top of a pile of cabbages in a cart bound for Rome. The driver, Pietro Fabri, delivered vegetables to the city twice a week, passing easily through the German checkpoints. Who better to smuggle Sam into the Eternal City?

As they reached the outskirts of the city, Sam was ordered to hide in the pile of cabbages, and they passed through without a problem. Fabri took Sam to a house near the markets, where a man was waiting for him. Aldo Zambardi suggested that Sam change his clothes, in order to look more like an Italian. But at six foot three inches, he was a rather unusual one: 'The trousers flapped above my ankles, the coat did not reach my knees and the little cap sat quaintly on the top of my head,' he recounted.

Zambardi hustled Sam onto a tram and ordered him to pretend to be asleep. That way, he would not have to speak to anyone and it be discovered that he was not Italian. There were many German officers on the train and so Sam tried to make himself as small as possible, not easy with his height and odd clothes. They held their breath until they got out at the Ponte Vittorio Emanuele II, one of the bridges across the River Tiber. In spite of his fear, Derry was astonished at the grandeur of St Peter's.

Keeping his eyes to the ground, he was ushered towards St Peter's Square, where a very tall priest, wearing a long black robe, stood just outside the basilica. As they approached him, the priest turned on his heel, muttering an instruction to follow him, several paces behind. To Sam's alarm, they seemed to be heading not towards the safety of St Peter's but away from it. His alarm deepened when he passed through a door where the words COLLEGIO TEUTONICO were inscribed in Latin. Did that not mean 'German college', he wondered. Still, he reasoned, he had little choice but to follow.

The priest led him into a sparsely furnished room, and revealed that he had been sending Sam money via the local country priest. And now, would Sam like a bath? This might seem an unusual offer, but Hugh knew how precious good clean water was to those on the run. And he was right: this would be Sam's first bath in a year and a half!

Clean, warm and dressed again, Sam waited until another man entered the room, stocky, middle-aged with dark hair. 'Major Derry, I believe.'

Sam was astonished. 'Does this go on all the time?' he asked the man, thinking of his journey to this place and the offer of a bath.

The man, who had introduced himself as John May – the Monsignor's fixer – laughed. 'Pretty nearly . . . never seems to rest – but I expect you'll get used to that, eventually. A wonderful character, the Monsignor.'

'The what?' Sam was astonished.

'Our Irish friend, the Right Reverend Monsignor Hugh O'Flaherty.'

'Oh, dear. That sounds damned important and I have been calling him Father all the time.'

'Never mind,' said John May. 'The Monsignor would be the last person to worry about that.'

Later that evening, Sam sat down to dinner, in the robes of a Monsignor, with Hugh and with D'Arcy Osborne, the British Minister. Hugh laughed at Sam's appearance. 'Not at all bad, me boy. You look more like a Monsignor than I do.'

It turned out that Sam's request for money and his credentials as the organiser of a network of escaped POWs intrigued Hugh O'Flaherty. And he needed the kind of help Sam was well placed to offer. But unlike Hugh, who trusted easily, D'Arcy needed to know more about this young British soldier. A coded message had been sent via the Foreign Office to Sam's home town in Nottinghamshire – was Sam Derry really who he said he was?

Sam was eager to prove his worth, assuring D'Arcy Osborne that he was genuine. 'Quite so, Major,' D'Arcy Osborne replied, but 'the Monsignor never checks up on anybody, he simply accepts at face value anyone who asks him for assistance . . . whatever the risk.' It was D'Arcy Osborne's job to protect Hugh as best he could.

Sam's story checked out. He was free to begin work putting a structure on the noble work Hugh had been doing. The British Escape Organisation, as it was called by that government, was founded in 1943, a formal organisation dedicated to helping the more than 1,000 escapees who had fled to Rome.

One day, Sam cheerfully told the Monsignor how pleased he was that this Irishman was so eager to help the British. Hugh quickly set him straight, talking about his childhood in Killarney under the rule of the British, and what had happened to his countrymen during that time.

The air was cleared, and Sam and Hugh got on

well from that time onwards. The Vatican produced an identity card for Sam: he was now Patrick Derry, an Irish writer employed by the Vatican. This ID card was vital to allow Sam to go anywhere in the city, as Ireland was not an enemy country, being neutral. But the Germans could check whether the ID was real at any moment ...

5 Ordinary Heroes

Hugh's first job was to introduce Sam Derry to the members of his organisation. He bustled through the streets of the city, a bundle of cheerful energy, with Sam following behind. 'If the distance was reasonable, we walked, partly because I needed the exercise but chiefly because the Monsignor liked walking,' Sam recalled. In any case, tram journeys were always worrying because the friendly locals would try to chat to Sam and it would become quickly obvious that he was not a Roman – and there were only so many times he could pretend to be asleep!

He was astonished at the size of Hugh's organisation and also just how ingenious many of Hugh's friends were. There was Brother Humilis, who was an expert in the black market, and managed to locate large amounts of food for the POWs in hiding. He tracked down a local man who made deliveries to the city – and extra ones in the false bottom of his cart. There was Count

Sarsfield Salazar at the Swiss Embassy, who channelled food and money to many of his countrymen outside Rome – until he was betrayed and had to flee the city into hiding. There were Hugh's priest friends, New Zealander Owen Sneddon and Fathers Claffey and Treacy, whose modest quarters were used as a 'clearing house' or temporary home for many escapees. And of course there was Henrietta Chevalier, Hugh's heroine, who had such a positive attitude to her work. 'They are absolutely grand, these boys,' she would say, 'They are just like my own children. It is all so marvellous.'

The reason Hugh was so successful in helping others was because of his great ability to make friends, such as the mysterious Mrs K, a German woman who was an expert in producing forged bread coupons, as all supplies were rationed during the War. A Madame Bruccoleri, who worked for the Red Cross, received many letters for POWs from their families at home, which she would pass on to Hugh O'Flaherty to give to those hiding in the city.

One of Hugh's greatest friends at this time was an Irishwoman, Delia Murphy. She was married to the Irish Minister Thomas Kiernan, who was strictly neutral in the War. Outgoing and sparky, just like Hugh, they were natural friends. And in spite of her position as the wife of a neutral minister, she knew whose side she was on. She had thought long and hard about how to help Hugh, but concluded that help she must:

'Around the city during the nine-month occupation of Rome, the Germans had splashed posters warning that anyone found sheltering an Allied prisoner of war would be shot. I doubt that they would have shot the wife of an Irish minister . . . I made sure that none of the high-ranking German warlords who invited the Kiernans to their feasts ever suspected what an Irish woman in Rome was doing during her spare time.'

The Case of the Disappearing Boots most certainly involved Delia. The garden of the Irish Legation backed on to a factory which repaired boots for German soldiers. This factory was not guarded at night, and over the course of a few weeks, boots began to disappear, thrown over the wall into the garden, where they were collected and passed on to Hugh. All the while, her husband was reporting back to the Irish government on the situation in Rome. He would also assure the Catholic Church in Ireland that those in the Vatican were still safe from the Germans – but not for long . . .

Of course, Hugh O'Flaherty's organisation sometimes found itself involved in shady matters. Even though Hugh had a fair idea what was going on, he also knew that Sam took care to ensure that he was not involved – after all, he was a priest. But Hugh was not quite as innocent as Sam thought. One day, a man called Peter Tumiati was introduced to Sam by Hugh. At the sight of this stranger, Sam held his breath: he was always on the look-out for German agents who had secretly gained access to the organisation. Did Hugh know Tumiati, he asked?

'Why, me boy, I know him well,' was the response. And indeed he did. What's more, Hugh knew exactly what Tumiati did: he was an agent, working for the British government. Tumiati was instructed to take back to the Allies in the south of Italy a list of all escaped POWs, 2,000 in all, so that their families could be assured they were safe. But he had to be careful. John May printed up the list on microfilm which was then hidden – in a loaf of bread!

Sometimes, there were worries about Hugh's safety. He insisted on roaming the streets and even visiting the dangerous Regina Coeli prison. 'It was quite difficult,' Sam said later, when recalling the risks Hugh took at this time. 'He was so charming and for his own safety, he couldn't care a damn . . . he still kept going around Rome although he had been told not to . . . he was in my opinion, taking unnecessary risks but, of course, he accepted no orders except from his superiors.'

One day, the Monsignor appeared with 'another new arrival for you, Patrick' (Patrick was Sam's alias in the Vatican). Sam was alarmed. The man standing in front of him was Pollak, a Jew who came from Czechoslovakia. When Sam had been imprisoned in Chieti and organising escapes, someone had given information to the Germans – and the finger of suspicion pointed at Joe Pollak.

Sam listened carefully to Joe's story. Joe explained that he had escaped with six others, including Sam's great friends John Furman and Bill Simpson. Sam reasoned that if they had trusted Joe, so must he. But when Joe brought John Furman to see Sam the next day, Sam took him to one side. Could he trust Joe Pollak?

'Joe Pollak is one of the most terrific chaps I have ever met,' was the reply. Not only had Joe helped others to escape, but he had found families willing to take them in. Because he was able to speak German, Hebrew, Greek, English and Italian, he was a natural leader of the escapees, who had made their way towards Rome to escape the frequent raids on farms in the countryside. Joe became a key member of Hugh's organisation.

6 Constant Danger

Hugh was a man who took risks to save lives. If others needed help, Hugh saw no obstacles, but would simply get on and do what was right. He was also a very good judge of character, and in Sam Derry he had chosen well.

Sam knew that one of his first tasks was to improve the organisation's security. Hugh had been, in his view, a little lax about it, using the words 'golf clubs' to refer to escapees and 'breviary' (a prayer book) to the accommodation which he would find for them.

Once Sam took charge, each key member of the organisation was given a code name. Hugh, given his love of the game, was called 'Golf', Sam was called 'Patrick', Father Anselmo Musters, 'Dutchpa', as he was a Dutch priest; Fr Sneddon became 'Horace', Henrietta Chevalier 'Mrs M', and, to his embarrassment, Count Salazar became 'Emma'.

Sam also organised a line of communication with the British government which allowed him to withdraw money to pay for food and accommodation, or 'billets' to use the military term, for the many who needed it. He also encouraged the escapees to behave themselves as befitted soldiers. To behave badly was to attract attention and to endanger the organisation in the process. One young soldier, Thorpe, was told, 'I have received a full report on your atrocious behaviour . . . I made a full report which has been sent to the proper authorities. You are to get out of Rome immediately.'

One of the first people to benefit from this new organisation was a Major Hugh Fane-Hervey, a tank commander in North Africa in 1942. His tank had come under fire and had burst into flames, trapping his gunner. Fane-Hervey managed to free the man and throw him clear. The enemy soldiers were so impressed that they gave him a round of applause. In spite of escaping once, Fane-Hervey was eventually captured and transferred to Frosinone in southern Italy. In this POW camp he met an old friend, Flight Lieutenant Garrad-Cole, and began to hatch an escape plan.

They both knew the Germans intended to take them north by train, to certain death. The Major somehow got hold of an axe and managed to conceal it in his trousers. The train rumbled through the country, stopping in Rome. Fane-Hervey and his friend started work, hacking away at the wooden wall of the train carriage. After a while, they were making good progress when, to their horror, the train started to move. They hacked away at the wall until a hole appeared, large enough for them to push through, 'a terrifying moment of hurtling through space,' as Garrad-Cole recalled. They hit the buffers below with a crash and rolled into the ditch, before stumbling off to hide.

The local villagers were friendly and helped them to buy tickets back to Rome where, Garrad-Cole says, 'I dreamed of sipping Chianti alongside unsuspecting storm troopers in a Roman café, of espionage, of beautiful Italian women. Little did I know . . .' The reality was undoubtedly far more dangerous.

When they reached Rome, Garrad-Cole was overwhelmed by the beauty of the Vatican, but knew that he and Fane-Hervey could not waste time on sightseeing. 'After a quick decision, we decided to approach the first benevolent-looking priest . . . picking one out, we walked up to him and Fane in his best Italian said, "We are British prisoners of war". The priest stopped in his tracks. His jaw dropped in amazement . . . then gathering his wits, he muttered. "I cannot help you . . . but wait here for half an hour . . ."'

True to his word, the priest returned with a man, who escorted them to the British Embassy. The man was Secundo Constantini, a key member of Hugh's organisation. Fane-Hervey and Garrad-Cole stayed there for ten days, during which time they amused themselves as best they could.

Escaped POW, Flight Lieutenant Garrad-Cole.

The embassy wine cellars were a real temptation to two bored soldiers. Through the locked cellar door, they could see champagne bottles on a shelf, tantalisingly out of reach. As Garrad-Cole recalled, 'the temptation was great, in fact, too great. We foraged around until we found a good stout curtain rod and to the end of this we fixed a piece of strong cord which we tied into a slip knot. Carefully we thrust the rod through the grille until the slip knot settled over the neck of the nearest champagne bottle. Gently, we removed the rod away until the slip knot was tight. Then gradually, we eased the bottle off the shelf . . .' Bottle after bottle was pulled through the grille in this way. That night, there was a party in the British Embassy.

A few days later, Secundo became aware that the embassy was being watched. Brother Robert Pace, a member of the organisation, code-named 'Whitebrows', was dispatched to move the two men. They found their way some days later to the apartment of two great friends of Hugh's, Renzo and Adrienne Lucidi, along with other British escapees, Bill Simpson and John Furman, who would become key members of the organisation.

Garrad-Cole had heard about Hugh O'Flaherty, the man responsible for his safety. Indeed, he remembered Hugh's visits to the prison camp when he was in Sulmona and how he had slipped them cigarettes when the camp guards weren't looking. He was anxious to meet and thank Hugh in person. He was shown to Hugh's room in the German College and was pleased to find many of Renzo and Adrienne's guests already there. 'We had an amusing tea party and I remember that the Monsignor produced a superb bottle of cognac for us before we left,' he reported happily. In these dangerous times, people celebrated whenever they could. Hugh knew how important it was to keep people's spirits up in such dark times. He was a welcoming and warm man, whose rooms were open to anyone who cared to visit. But more than that, as Lieutentant Garrad-Cole discovered, Hugh was a modest man. He didn't seek acclaim for the work he was doing, content to let others find him, to show leadership to those who needed it without demanding anything in return. For Hugh, the safety of those in his care was all that mattered.

7 Essential Supplies

Bill Simpson was astonished at the scene which greeted him and his two friends, John Furman and Joe Pollak, when they visited Henrietta Chevalier's flat just before Christmas. She introduced them to her two daughters, Gemma and Mary, who had been screaming at each other, and to her mother, peeling vegetables in the kitchen. Altogether, there were seven women in the house. 'Some family,' Bill said, confused.

'Oh, that's not all,' said Mrs Chevalier, leading the three to another door. She pushed it open. Four men lay in one huge bed, their faces turned to the visitors. 'Good morning,' said the four in unison. As 'Mrs M' introduced Bill to her four private escapees, they climbed out of bed, fully dressed. 'They hop into bed every time someone comes close to the door,' she explained.

The three friends were there to see if they could help with the distribution of food to all the escapees in the city. Henrietta's flat, as well as housing POWs, was also a depot for food supplies. Hugh provided money for fruit and vegetables; a friend, Giovanni, provided meat and got his friends to buy sugar and other scarce items from the black market. A friendly baker provided her with bread without needing the precious coupons provided by the authorities.

But the distribution of food was more of a problem, Henrietta explained. Carrying large suitcases only attracted attention, as the police were on the look-out for black marketeers. Sometimes Father Borg took supplies, sometimes Brother Robert, or even the girls, when no one else was available, but it was simply too dangerous. One of Bill's first jobs was to hire someone to transport the food through the city. A local man had a horse-drawn carriage and was paid to distribute the food and the system worked well even though every week, fewer and fewer food items were available. Tea and coffee could not be found, bread was scarce and the prices on the black market were very high.

A natural leader, who inspired others with his energy and good humour, Hugh had chosen his trusty lieutenants well. In the short time that he had been in charge, Sam had made many good changes to Hugh's organisation, and Bill, John and Joe were real assets to Hugh. They were able to move around the city fairly easily, as their forged papers were good enough to convince the authorities and each spoke Italian fairly well. But John Furman wondered why more people weren't being hidden in the Vatican – after all, wasn't it safe from the Germans? Sam explained to him that firstly it would compromise Hugh: 'The Monsignor would get it in the neck from the Vatican authorities . . . he is already highly suspect and we have good reason to believe he stands pretty high on the Gestapo blacklist.' The second reason was more sinister: 'So far, the Germans haven't worried over-much about the Vatican . . . if we start filling it up with escapers, there's obviously going to be a reaction.' Perhaps the Germans would not honour their promise not to invade the Holy City much longer . . .

But the Vatican was in more immediate danger, and not from the Germans. Italian Resistance to the German occupation of Rome was beginning to gather strength. On the evening of 18 December 1943, the Resistance bombed a favourite haunt of Nazis and Fascists, killing eight German soldiers. The next night, the Resistance attacked the Hotel Floria, headquarters of the German High Command. Casualties were heavy.

The Germans cracked down in response. The curfew – which had prevented Romans from going out after 11.30 at night – was changed to seven o'clock, after which the streets were to be emptied. There was a ban on bicycles, often used by the Resistance for their attacks. The warning was stark: 'The use of any bicycle anywhere in the territory of the open city of Rome is prohibited. Transgressors [those who disobeyed the

Lieutenant Colonel Herbert Kappler, who was head of the Gestapo in Rome during the Second World War.

Pietro Koch, Chief of the Fascist police squad in Rome.

ruling] will be shot without regard to who they are and without prior notice.'

However, the ingenious Romans simply added a wheel or two from prams to their bicycles, making them into tricycles, which were not banned – although, after a few days, these were forbidden, too.

But events took an even more sinister turn. Pietro Koch was to lead a new Italian Fascist police squad and the numbers of German security forces began to grow by the day. Hugh's boss, Monsignor Montini, began to worry – could this be a sign that Pietro Koch and his group would dare invade the Vatican? Only days later, Montini's suspicions were proved right.

The notice on the door of the Basilica of San Giovanni was in Italian and German. It said that all searches were prohibited because the church belonged to the Vatican. But more importantly, more than 200 people were in hiding there, some of Italy's leading anti-Fascists and more than 50 Jews. On 21 December, there was a banging on the door and Pietro Koch and his Fascist soldiers burst in. Many of the men in hiding had been expecting a raid, and fled, but others were not so lucky. And they could not pretend that they were seminarians, or trainee priests either. Pietro Koch had thought of that. In his gang was a man who had once been a monk and he set them a test. He asked each and every captured man to recite the Ave Maria: if he did not know the prayer, he could not possibly be a priest. Eighteen men were captured.

It was clear that the Germans were prepared to bend the rules to capture their prey, using Koch to disguise their own involvement in the raids. In public, though, they cracked down even harder on ordinary Roman citizens. Anyone sheltering POWs or owning a wireless transmitter would be executed. Anyone who even made contact with POWs or printed anything negative about the Germans, even taking photographs outdoors, would be sentenced to hard labour for life.

And Pietro Koch was more dangerous than the Germans, in many ways. As an Italian, he was closer to the ground and had a network of informers, people who were ready to betray their fellow Romans for food or money. His network had also tracked down a number of radio transmitters in the city, one of which was located in Via dell'Impero, where Mrs Chevalier lived.

One winter afternoon, Paul Chevalier called to see his mother, Henrietta. But it was not a social visit. He was there to warn her that the German security forces would raid the area that evening. It was time for her 'guests' to scatter throughout the city.

At seven o'clock, the building's porter, Edigio, knocked quietly on her door. The Germans were coming. Moments later, a much louder knock on the door announced the arrival of SS troopers, who searched each of the rooms and asked Henrietta about the size of her family, unable to believe that seven women lived in this tiny apartment. There was no way, they reasoned, that anyone else could possibly fit into this cramped space. Gemma Chevalier held her breath as one of the soldiers rummaged in a pile of gramophone records, sighing with relief when he missed the English disc amongst them. The soldiers left, having found nothing. By nine o'clock that night, the seven women and their POW guests were eating supper.

But danger was never far away during this time. Kappler, the Commander of the Gestapo in Rome, had been given more soldiers and Pietro Koch was more determined than ever to root out anti-Fascists, and their grip tightened on the city. A plain-clothes member of Koch's gang could be seen more or less every day from the window of the Chevaliers' apartment and one day, Gemma Chevalier had a close shave. She was sent to buy cigarettes in a local shop for the guests. As she handed over the money, there was a curious expression on the shopkeeper's face and she noticed an Italian man watching her. She knew that she couldn't go home in case he would follow her, so she walked the other way. His footsteps rang louder behind her as she hurried along the streets. She knew that she had to shake him off somehow. Seeing a tram approaching, she seized her chance. She dashed across the tracks, right in the path of the tram. Onlookers were horrified, thinking she had been struck, but when the tram passed, all that remained were cigarettes, scattered all over the street. There was no trace of the girl. The man turned on his heel and walked away. Needless to say, Gemma kept the news of her narrow escape from her mother.

As Christmas approached, the raids by Pietro Koch and the Fascist police became more daring. Unlike the SS, they made raids on many houses that belonged to the Vatican. They picked the Holy City as a particular target, enraged that the Vatican refused to recognise their government. Mother Mary St Luke recorded a raid on the Oriental Institute, run by the Jesuits, where they were sheltering three Jews. 'The brother porter faced the Fascists and said, "You have no right here, this is Pontifical Property, where are your papers?"

"Here," was the answer and the Brother found himself looking into the muzzle of a revolver.'

The Fascists would capture two of the Jews hiding there, the first a man who collapsed with heart problems, the second, his friend who refused to leave him to his fate. They were both taken away.

8 Christmas 1943

Even though the situation in the city was tense, Hugh O'Flaherty insisted that Christmas was to be celebrated. By this stage, he and his organisation were looking after 2,000 people, and Hugh was determined that each one of them would get something to remind them of the season. He filled his room in the German College with hundreds of small parcels, each cheerily wrapped by his friend Molly Stanley, and enlisted the help of a small army of priests to carry the presents all through the city.

Bill and his friend John Furman distributed turkeys, wine, cigarettes and Molly's presents, and on Christmas Day, they gathered in Mrs Chevalier's tiny apartment to toast the season, crammed with British 'guests', food and presents. On St Stephen's Day everyone gathered in Hugh's rooms, where a procession of priests, diplomats and other odd guests turned up to say hello and to join in a sing-song, led by the Irish Ambassador's wife, Delia

Molly Stanley, the tiny Englishwoman who was a friend and helper of Hugh O'Flaherty.

Lieutenants Bill Simpson (left) and John Furman (right), both escaped POWs who became key members of the Rome Escape Organisation.

Murphy, a famous singer. Father 'Spike' Buckley was a fine singer, too, as John Furman noted with amusement. 'Spike, when mellowed with wine would sing sentimental Irish ballads to order.'

As usual, Hugh knew just what was needed and his Christmas celebrations were a great ray of light during these dark times. With life becoming more difficult in Rome by the day, people knew that they had to enjoy themselves when they could.

The authorities took a census of the population in Rome, to force people on the run from their hiding places. An astonishing 100,000 Italian soldiers, 3,000 POWs and several hundred Jews were estimated to be hiding in the city at this time. And what better way to rout them out than to restrict food? Only those whose names were listed on the census paper would get food tickets. And food was in very short supply in the city: in November, no butter, sugar or rice had arrived in the city and whilst people grew their own vegetables, with fighting coming ever closer to the city, their crops would end up being destroyed. The situation in Rome was at crisis point. And with this crisis would come great danger for Hugh's organisation.

Even though escaped POWs were on the run from the Germans, they did not have to hide away in their 'billets' all the time. Providing their papers were in order, and they had a story ready for any curious German officer, they could wander freely through the city. Some even took to going to Rome's famous opera. Indeed, on New Year's Day 1944, Bill Simpson and John Furman were in the audience for Puccini's *Tosca*, along with Captain Pip Gardner and Lieutenant Colonel 'Tug' Wilson, and their great friends Adrienne and Renzo Lucidi, surrounded by German uniforms. On seeing that one of the Germans was a high-ranking officer, Adrienne leaned forward in her seat and smiled at him. Using all her charm she enquired if the officer would be so kind as to autograph her programme. Flattered, the officer obliged, signing with a flourish, unaware that his signature might be copied in many forged documents.

Other POWs, such as Garrad-Cole, were even bolder in their movements. 'There were plenty of German soldiers in the streets,' he noted on one of his rambles around the city. 'Most of them seemed to be sight-seeing and were probably on Christmas leave from the front in the south. They paid no regard to me when I stood alongside them admiring the beauties of Rome and this encouraged me to get over the feeling of being a fugitive on the run.' He relied on friendly Romans too, who would be willing to give them food and drink, knowing that they were escaped POWs. In one bar, the POWs could order 'schnapps' like the German soldiers, and a bottle of whiskey would be produced from under the counter.

Hugh's allies and supporters had become experts at getting what they needed for their escapees, particularly the papers which would guarantee their safety in the city. Many of these papers were expert forgeries, but were not a match for genuine papers. One day, John May, Hugh's great fixer, just happened to be passing when a pile of passes for Vatican officials was being submitted to the German ministry for signature and the official stamp. Into this pile, he slipped three 'new' passes, for Simpson, Furman and Pollak. When he returned some time later, genuine passes for these three 'Vatican employees' had been signed by the German ministry. They were like gold dust to these key members of Hugh's organisation.

Nonetheless, the tension which had prevailed before Christmas became ever greater as the Germans and the Fascists became bolder. Worse, there had been a security breach around the Sulmona prison camp. Eighteen Italians had been arrested and who knew what they might tell the German authorities about the activities of Hugh O'Flaherty? The situation was grave. Bill Furman and Renzo Lucidi, along with a French escapee, Henri Payonne, had come to warn the Monsignor to be careful. Just before curfew, Payonne was sent away, clutching Renzo Lucidi's telephone number in his hand. He was told on no account to give it to anyone, not even to his good friend Iride Imperioli, one of the organisation's key helpers at Sulmona.

9 Betrayal

Early that morning, the telephone rang in Renzo's flat. It was Iride calling from Sulmona. She told Joe Pollak that she must see him at once. Joe wondered if it was a trap. He debated the consequences of going to see her, when she rang him twice more, each time imploring him to come. The telephone rang for a fourth time and Adrienne Lucidi, who was there with Joe, answered it. But the person on the line was not Iride – it was Henri Payonne. Everyone was in danger and should get out at once, he said. In the commotion, Adrienne did not grasp the other warning, that Joe was on no account to keep his appointment with Iride.

They gathered together their belongings and cleared out, rushing to meet Hugh and Sam Derry. They didn't know if the call was genuine or a fake. Hugh was convinced that it was a trap, but Joe Pollak thought that he must see Iride – it was the only way to find out what was going on, one way or another. He left at noon, and agreed that if he had not returned by four o'clock, they would know he had fallen into a trap.

At four o'clock that afternoon, there was a knock at the door to the building. Someone was sent downstairs to open it, to find a young Italian boy standing there, clutching a note in his hand. The note was for Patrick Derry only – Sam's false name. Should Derry go down to the boy? Again, they wondered if it was genuine, or another trap. As Sam's Italian was poor and no one wanted to implicate the Monsignor, John Furman was sent. Persuading the boy to part with the note, he opened it to discover the worst. Iride Imperioli had been captured, along with her mother, her sister and her baby and was afraid that 'Giuseppe', the code name for Joe, might talk if he thought he had been betrayed. 'I won't talk unless threatened that I endanger the life of my baby by not doing so,' the bleak note said. 'They only want to know who supplies the money and I repeat that they will never know from me – I prefer death.'

But it was too late. Joe Pollak had boarded a train from Rome to Sulmona, and walked briskly to Iride's boarding house. Immediately when he rounded the corner to the building, he sensed that he was in danger. Someone was waiting for him. He made a run for it, pursued through the streets before dashing into a building and begging the porter in Italian. 'I am an escaped British soldier. Please help me.'

Taking one look at this small, dark man who spoke excellent Italian and wore civilian clothes, the porter replied, 'And I'm the Pope.'

It was too late for Iride and Joe, who were taken to Sulmona POW camp by their German captors. But how much did the Germans know about Hugh's organisation? Iride knew the most about his activities and so it was vital that she not talk. Hugh took heart from the fact that the Germans had simply taken Joe and Iride back to the camp, and had not yet interrogated them. But he decided that the apartment on Via Chelini should be cleared out.

But then the story took another twist. During the morning of 8 January, two Gestapo officers, dressed in civilian clothes, paid a visit to a widow whose son was in Regina Coeli prison. They told her that they were in the Italian Resistance and that they were trying to help her son to escape from prison, where he was being constantly tortured. They wanted her help to spring him from captivity, by gathering together his supporters to mount an ambush on the prison.

In her innocence, the widow believed them, even though it was a plot to capture the Communists, whom the Gestapo considered an enemy. And so she took them to meet the Resistance leader, Nabolante, who was also one of Hugh's great helpers. Nabolante was sheltering Pip Gardner and Tug Wilson, and within moments, the Gestapo had arrested all three of them. They left behind some SS men in uniform with Nabolante's cook, an old man who was terribly frightened. This old man knew of the apartments on Via Firenze and Via Chelini and even more dangerously, the secret code to the doorbell of each apartment.

Hugh ordered John Furman to clear the apartment on Via Firenze. He hurried along and let himself into the flat. Soon, there was a ring on the doorbell and when John opened it, Nabolante's cook was standing there, along with two suspicious-looking men. He did not like the look of the cook's two companions. They did not seem to him to be individuals who would go out of their way to help anyone. John was right. When he asked the two men for proof of their identities, they pulled not identity cards but revolvers from their pockets and half a dozen SS men, armed to the teeth, poured in.

Furman was immediately arrested, along with five officers, two privates, one American Air Force sergeant, a Yugoslav helper, Bruno Buchner, and Herta, an Austrian girl who did the housekeeping. Furman knew that Bill Simpson was due at the apartment at any minute. He hoped and prayed that he wouldn't turn up. Furman heard the doorbell stutter and stop. 'It sounded as though there might be a faulty connection,' he later recalled. 'Another soldier asked my guard "Did the bell ring then?" . . . One of the soldiers walked slowly to the door and opened it.' There was no one there.

Bill had rung the doorbell and had been standing outside the flat, on the first-floor landing, when he had been distracted by the building porter waving frantically from her room, urging him not to go any further. He vanished, just in time to see the flat door open and a German soldier come out and start to fiddle with the bell.

As soon as the coast was clear, Simpson made a run for it. Half an hour later, he reached St Peter's and ran all the way up to the now-familiar room, where he found Sam and the Monsignor. 'Chelini's had it! And John along with it,' he blurted out. Their faces fell.

Hugh knew that the consequences of this security breach could be fatal, particularly for Bruno and Herta, who would be considered traitors by the Germans. Perhaps the Nazis would even try to raid the Monsignor's quarters. 'Just let them try it!' interrupted the Monsignor with a grim expression. 'If any of these scoundrels ever dare to come near this room, I will beat the . . .' Hugh was serious, but he had no real protection should there be a raid. His only tool was a coil of rope which he hid under his bed and which he could use to climb out the window and down to the courtyard below.

On his way to Regina Coeli prison, John Furman managed to tear up his identity papers and his notebook with the coded addresses and telephone numbers of Hugh's organisation into tiny fragments. He pushed them, one by one, out of the lorry. At least this way, further secrets would not be betrayed.

10 Desperate Measures

It was vital that the security of all the billets be checked and Hugh organised a group of priests to fan out throughout the city, checking on the many private homes and apartments in which escapees had been hidden, to ensure that all were safe. The priests had Vatican passes and so did not have to observe the strict seven o'clock curfew. They worked through the night, visiting their charges and keeping an eye out for the SS or for Pietro Koch's men.

The task of visiting the Via Firenze apartment, the most dangerous one, was reserved for Father Owen Sneddon. He did not realise that the cook had also led the SS to this apartment and that all in it had been captured, but approached it with caution nonetheless. As he did, he caught sight of the building's Italian porter who made a face at him to tell him that all was not well. He walked on by.

All the other billets were safe, but from now on, it was decided, it was important that no one know too much about the organisation's activities. The only people who had the complete picture were Sam, Hugh and Bill Simpson. But Herr Kappler had a pretty good idea too . . .

One day, Hugh received an invitation to a reception at the Hungarian Embassy. Hugh knew what this meant: the Germans often used the embassy for informal gatherings. He also knew that in order to attend the reception, he would have to leave the haven of his rooms and the safety of the Vatican – could the invitation be a trap?

Ever courageous, Hugh decided to take a chance. At the reception, he was approached by Von Weizsaecker, the German Ambassador. He was not a Nazi sympathiser, but had a job to do all the same. The warning was friendly, but clear. The Germans knew exactly what Hugh was up to. 'If you ever step outside Vatican territory again, on whatever pretext, you will be arrested at once,' Von Weizsaecker told him. 'Now, will you please think about what I've said?'

Hugh, a great deal taller than the Ambassador, smiled down at him and said, in a loud voice, 'Your Excellency is too considerate. I will certainly think about what you've said . . . sometimes.'

It seemed that the organisation was coming under pressure from many quarters. Hugh's boss, Montini, also had a quiet word. The Germans had complained to him about Hugh's activities and from now on he was to stay inside the Vatican. 'I had my knuckles rapped pretty hard,' he would say later. But it is clear that Montini did not ask him to stop his work with the POWs. After all, if he had really wanted Hugh to stop, he could have given him a direct order, or sent him to another country, out of harm's way.

Sam Derry was also to receive an order. One morning, Hugh turned up at Sam's office in the Vatican. 'This time, it's marching orders for you, me boy,' he said. 'Would you believe it, now, the Rector has just informed me that he has reason to believe that the gentleman who is a guest in my room is not a neutral Irishman at all.' They both knew that the Rector was not a Nazi sympathiser, but had clearly been pressured to turn Sam out of his quarters. But they also knew that if he left the Vatican, it would only be a matter of time before he was picked up. And so, on 12 January 1944, Sam put on Hugh's clerical habit once more, the black hat and cloak, and set off for his new home, in the office of the British Minister, D'Arcy Osborne.

But others were not to be as lucky as Sam. Bruno and Herta had no Vatican protection. As Hugh reported, 'He said he was going to be shot this morning. He wanted me to know that he never opened his mouth once. Well, I got a message an hour ago. Bruno's dead. They shot him this morning.' Herta was sentenced to five years' imprisonment and taken to Austria to serve it. It was clear that the consequences for helping Hugh's organisation could be deadly.

The raids on the apartments of Hugh's sympathisers continued. One day, the young Italian boy appeared at Henrietta Chevalier's door to tell her that a raid was about to take place. Should she believe him? She wasn't sure, but her five guests, mindful of the fact that Hugh had told them that Henrietta was to be protected at all costs, decided to go with the boy. Within ten minutes, the Gestapo knocked on her door.

Of course, they found nothing but an ordinary, tiny family flat in which no one, apart from Henrietta and her family, could possibly have lived. The Gestapo officer asked her if she knew who might have given him this information. Henrietta suspected that her neighbours, Fascist sympathisers, might have been responsible. Well, she told the Gestapo officer, she *had* seen some strangers going in and out of that apartment . . . She pointed to the neighbour's front door and for the next half an hour, listened with satisfaction to the noisy search of their apartment.

But Bill Simpson knew that it was time Henrietta thought of her own safety and that her lodgers would have to go elsewhere for the time being. Little did Bill know, but he would have to heed his own advice. He was staying with Renzo and Adrienne Lucidi, two of Hugh's greatest supporters, and Lieutenant Fane-Hervey, along with a Polish explosives expert, Rafaelo, who had carefully stored one of his bags of gelignite at the flat.

It was late at night when a loud knock at the door startled them all from sleep. They only just had time to hide the gelignite and order Simpson to act the part of Renzo and Adrienne's nephew. The Gestapo marched in and began to search the flat, demanding everyone's papers. Fortunately, Bill's papers declared him to be Guglielmo del Monte and the officers believed him. They left the apartment and everyone breathed a sigh of relief. Rafaelo and Fane-Hervey made a run for it.

Then the Gestapo came back: they had forgotten to check Fane-Hervey's papers. Quickly, Renzo's son Gerald made up a story about how Fane-Hervey had come to play cards and had stayed the night, but had less success in persuading them why he had an issue of a Communist Party newspaper in his bedroom. He was arrested, and only released at the request of the French Ambassador, as Gerald had been born in France.

The arrests of Hugh's key helpers continued. Concetta Piazza, a nurse living north of Rome, was the link between Hugh and two dozen POWs hiding out in caves in the countryside. She had just finished delivering food and money to them when she was arrested. Even though she had no evidence on her, she was taken to Regina Coeli prison and charged with helping Allied escapees.

But Concetta was not to be scared that easily. On a piece of toilet paper, she wrote a long letter – to none other than Field Marshal Kesselring, Commander of the German forces in Italy. She had done a lot of good work for her patients, whether they be Allies or Germans, and in prison she could not do this valuable job, she wrote. She persuaded a prisoner who was being released to smuggle the letter out. Of course, it found its way to Hugh O'Flaherty, who had it typed up for her. Hugh then thought for a while. The letter needed to go to Von Weiszaecker, but who could be relied upon to deliver it to him? Dr Kiernan, the Irish Ambassador, was the obvious choice. The letter was dispatched, marked for the personal attention of Field Marshal Kesselring. Two days later, Concetta Piazza was released.

Hugh was lucky to have some brave and resourceful people working in his organisation, but the work was clearly becoming more and more dangerous. The Fascist circle was closing around Hugh's helpers. Pietro Koch was now joined by Pietro Caruso, the new Fascist Chief of Police, 'Full of zeal for his new office and burning to show the republic what he can do in support of it,' as Mother Mary St Luke noted in her diary.

Koch and Caruso began to plan a major series of raids, with the Vatican as the main target. On 3 February 1944, one of Koch's gang began to knock on the ancient carved doors of St Paul Outside-the-Walls, one of the four great papal basilicas of the city, founded by the Emperor Constantine. He knocked loudly and frantically, shouting for help. When it came and the door was opened, Pietro Caruso and his gang stormed into the beautiful building. Sixty-six people were arrested, including nine Jews. The Vatican protested but the Germans denied any involvement.

But the Vatican was growing increasingly concerned. At this stage 55 monasteries, 100 convents and many other Vatican properties were hiding Jews, as many as 4,500 of them, working quietly away in the Vatican library or for the Palatine Guard. From 1942 until 1943, membership of the Guard – and automatic Vatican citizenship – mysteriously increased from 200 to more than 4,000 . . .

The situation in Rome was growing more tense by the day. At the same time, the Allies were mounting a daring attack on the south of the country. Would Rome be liberated before long?

11 A False Dawn

On 22 January 1944, the citizens of Rome received great news, as Mother Mary St Luke noted in her diary. 'During the night the Allies made a landing at Anzio . . . it seems too good to be true . . . people in the streets look happier than they have for a long time.' She was right. It *was* too good to be true.

On the morning of 22 January, 50,000 American troops and 5,000 vehicles landed at the beaches of Anzio, a seaside town only 30 miles from Rome. There, they met no Germans at all. It would seem that they had taken them completely by surprise. The Allies were jubilant. But this joy turned to dismay as the Allied Commander, instead of pushing forward towards Rome, stayed put. As the British Prime Minister Winston Churchill put it, 'I had hoped that we were hurling a wildcat on the shore, but all we got was a stranded whale.'

By the time the Commander was ready to move forward, the Germans had regrouped and what should have been a strong push northwards turned into a long and deadly battle, lasting for four months and costing the lives of thousands. The Allies were determined to win out, though, bombing the ancient and beautiful monastery of Monte Cassino which, they argued, contained German weapons. But when the abbot of the monastery came to Rome to report, he said that there were no weapons. The Vatican wondered if Rome might be next. Rome had been declared an 'open city' after the Allied bombing in 1943, with the Germans agreeing not to retaliate, in order to preserve the city's beautiful buildings. But who knew what they might do now, if they were forced to defend themselves?

As the front lines crept nearer to Rome, Hugh's escape organisation faced even more danger. Sam worried about POWs, hopeful of liberation, coming out into the open too soon and being recaptured. With the Germans on the run and beginning to panic, they would almost certainly be shot immediately. Bill Simpson was given his orders: the escapees were to stay hidden.

For John Furman, in Regina Coeli prison, liberation could not come soon enough. A note was passed to him one day, telling him that on 26 January, all the British prisoners were to be taken from the jail, to where they did not know. But he did know that he was probably going to his death. He wrote to his good friend Sam, telling him, 'If I fail to make it, I know that you will see my wife and Diana [his daughter] when you get back. Would you also ask Bill to remember me to all my friends who have been so kind to me ...' He also asked if Bill would remember him to 'our Irish golfing friend,' a code for Hugh, who was a keen golfer.

Just like Sam Derry, John was loaded onto a train going north, towards certain death. And just like Sam, he knew that he had to jump. Risking everything, he flung himself off the train. He managed to find a bicycle and, even though he was only a few miles from the Swiss border and safety in that neutral country, he and his friend Johnny Johnstone cycled all the way down to Rome, 400 miles away, so that he could see his old friend Hugh once more.

'I felt happy and suddenly relaxed as I watched Johnny's enchanted eyes taking in the beauty of the square, the colonnade, the obelisk, the fountains, the Swiss Guards and the Basilica itself. Rather self-consciously, we shook hands.' John was home again.

With the help of a friendly priest, John got word to Hugh that he had returned. Astonished, Hugh greeted his friend, slapping his back and enveloping him in a bear hug. 'In the name of God, it is good to see you back, John. You are paler and thinner but you are in one piece. This is surely a happy day for us all.'

One of the first people John was anxious to see was Sam Derry. It would be consolation for having got a very sore bottom after the long cycle, to see his old friend again, he joked. But Sam knew better than to come out into the open and meet John. If he was spotted, it could put the whole organisation, and the British government, in danger. John's one consolation was that he and Bill Simpson became a team again.

Some months later, another old friend from the past would also reappear, Joe Pollak. He had managed to escape from Sulmona prison camp, at the very moment when he was being transported to Germany and certain death. He had been taken to the train station at Aquila, ready to board the train. Suddenly, there was a huge explosion: the train station was being bombed. Seizing his chance, Joe made a run for it. As he could speak Italian fluently, he managed to hitch a lift in a lorry heading for Rome. Joe thought he was safe, until he saw the German checkpoint ahead. Thinking quickly, he slipped over the side of the truck and crawled underneath. He could hear nothing but discussions in German and Italian and worked out that the driver was being arrested. Suddenly, the lorry was driving off again, with a terrified Joe clinging to the underside. He knew that they must be heading to the nearest German barracks and that, somehow, he needed to get off. To his relief, the van slowed down at a sharp bend and he dropped off.

He headed towards Rome and Via Chelini, unaware that it was no longer safe. What's more, the man who had rented it for Hugh, a Doctor Cipolla, was a suspected double agent. And so, when Joe turned up, he could easily have been walking into another trap. But Dr Cipolla was anxious to get into Hugh's good books again, and did not betray Joe. Perhaps, they thought, he wasn't a double agent after all.

12 Taking Risks

There were lots of challenges facing Hugh: how to keep the POWs safe and fed, but also what to do if they were sick. Henrietta Chevalier had some nursing experience and, together with an escaped Yugoslavian doctor, Milko Scofic, travelled the city looking after those escapees in need of medical treatment. But sometimes a prisoner needed hospital treatment and this could be very dangerous.

Private Norman Anderson was hiding on a farm 40 miles north of Rome. One day he was doubled over with pain, and it was discovered that he had acute appendicitis. If he didn't get treatment, he would die. Brother Pace, who was looking after him, told him that the only option was to leave him at a hospital, even if he risked being recaptured. But Norman refused – death was preferable, in his view.

Hugh, as usual, came to the rescue. He contacted an old friend of his, Professor Urbani, a surgeon in one of the

Roman hospitals. Would he treat Norman? This might seem like a simple request, but the hospital was full of German wounded from the battle at Anzio, who would surely notice the stranger among them. The professor agreed, but Norman would have to be smuggled in and back out again before anyone noticed.

In a daring plan, Hugh got his friend Father 'Spike' Buckley to help, heaving the young man over his shoulder. Delia Murphy drove Norman to the hospital in the Irish official car, a huge risk. Even though the car was protected by diplomatic plates, the Gestapo could still ask questions of the driver.

Within an hour of his operation, Norman was whisked out of the hospital, still seriously ill. He was placed gently into the car and Delia and Spike set off again, driving through the streets of Rome. After a while, they breathed a sigh of relief. They were safe. They stopped at a set of traffic lights and were startled by a loud rapping on the car window. Father Buckley wound it down to greet the two SS men standing outside. The man in the back of the car was a priest, he explained, and they were taking him to hospital. Norman looked so bad that the two SS men waved them on. Norman would recover in the care of Henrietta Chevalier.

One of the men Hugh helped, Major Gambier-Perry, had been baffled by this ragtag organisation, so unlike his own military one. He puzzled over 'The strangeness of this organisation in which soldiers and

Delia Murphy, singer and wife of the Irish Minister, Thomas Kiernan.

priests, diplomats and communists, noblemen and humble working folk, were all operating in concord, with a single aim and yet without any clearly defined pyramid of authority.'

This looseness reflected Hugh's nature, to make connections with others, to trust in their bravery and to let them be resourceful, and to shun hierarchy. He was also a man prepared to take risks in order to help others. Sometimes very big risks.

Tom Carini was one of the leaders of the Italian Resistance, and was in Santo Spirito Hospital. He was ill and had been tortured by Pietro Koch, leader of the Fascist police. He was guarded at all times by two armed police, and knew that if he tried to escape, he would be executed at once. His mother begged the nuns, who were in charge of the hospital, to help him escape and they agreed.

The nuns had noticed that at 2 a.m. every night, one of the guards couldn't help nodding off, overcome by the need to sleep in the middle of a long and boring night.

One night, the Mother Superior seized her chance. Tom Carini woke at 2 a.m., with the strangest sensation that his feet were being tickled. And they were – to his astonishment he looked up and saw none other than the Mother Superior at the end of his bed. Signalling to him to be absolutely quiet, she smuggled him out of the room, under the nose of the sleeping guard. He was taken to the nuns' dormitory, where the habit of a Monsignor lay waiting for him, provided by Hugh. Tom sat with the Mother Superior and recited the rosary until, at dawn, Hugh arrived. Moments later two tall men, dressed in long cloaks and the distinctive hats of Monsignors, left the hospital and vanished into the streets.

13 No End in Sight

It was now spring 1944, and the winter had not been kind to Hugh's operation. It had been a long and bitter winter, and many of those hiding in the country could no longer bear the cold and hunger and came to Rome for help. But Rome was no longer a place to hide safely, and as quickly as they were helped, they were sent back to the countryside. Each day, a new wave of desperate and needy people arrived, and Hugh helped every single one of them, even though he was no longer able to leave the Vatican.

By now, his organisation was helping 3,423 escapees, including 400 Russians, in 200 billets, at a cost of around £10,000 pounds – which would nowadays be around €400,000. As one admiring American put it, 'He was the good angel of all escaped prisoners . . . this worthy man risked his life for all of us, day after day.'

The case of Paul Freyberg, a young lieutenant in the Grenadier Guards, would demand every bit of

Hugh's skill and ingenuity. Paul had been captured at Anzio, but had managed to escape and make his way into the countryside. There he met an Italian man, who had spent some time in America and was a fluent English speaker. This man offered Paul civilian clothes and urged him to make for the papal summer palace of Castel Gandolfo. Some days later, Paul appeared at the door of the palace, seeking shelter on Vatican property.

The Vatican was rather at a loss what to do, because Paul Freyberg was no ordinary soldier. He was the son of General Freyberg, one of the key commanders of the Allied Forces, who had taken Crete from the Germans. If word got out that the Vatican was actively helping an Allied soldier, and one so important, it could be very embarrassing for them. Paul Freyberg needed to be spirited out of Castel Gandolfo and fast. And who better to organise this than Hugh O'Flaherty?

There was one problem. Between the castle and Rome lay a large number of German soldiers. Hugh had an idea. The truck which carried supplies from Rome to the villa was never checked – the Germans were used to its movements and knew that it was simply carrying food. But on this day, the truck would carry some extra cargo. Paul was astonished to see that a small hollow space had been made in the middle of the truck which was piled high with sacks of potatoes and crates of garden produce. Lined with sacking, this cavity was to hold Paul on his way to Rome. Paul Freyberg celebrated his twenty-first birthday in the British Legation in Rome, surrounded by new friends. At this party, Sam Derry was delighted to bump into John Furman once again.

But as Hugh became more daring in his efforts to help POWs, the Germans became more determined than ever to capture Hugh. And they were no longer willing to wait for him to set foot outside the Vatican. They decided to see if they could lure him away.

One day, an Italian peasant, a man who came into the city every day with supplies, was captured by the Gestapo and tortured. The Gestapo knew that this man often supplied Hugh's organisation. He would have his freedom, they told him, if he would lure Hugh out of the Vatican. 'Tell him that someone needs help,' the peasant was ordered.

Fearing for his life, the man agreed. He sent a message to Hugh saying that he needed to see him. Of course, Hugh waited for him at his usual place, at the top of the steps in St Peter's Square. It was only eight o'clock in the morning, and the square was quiet. As the man approached, Hugh caught sight of the Gestapo car, parked just beside the white boundary line which divided the Vatican from the city of Rome. There were three men in the car and the engine was running. The peasant walked across the square towards Hugh, looking over his shoulder at the car behind him. Twice he passed Hugh, without looking at him, circling his prey. On the third and final time, he looked Hugh in the eye, and made a run for it down a side street. Hugh breathed a sigh of relief. John May, who had come with him, dismissed the Swiss Guards who were waiting to see if the Germans would be bold enough to cross the boundary.

But the Germans were not willing to give up. They captured another of Hugh's helpers, a man called Grossi, who looked after some of Hugh's escaped POWs in his flat. Again, they tortured him to betray Hugh. Then Kappler had a plan. Grossi's flat would not be raided, so Hugh would not be aware that there was anything amiss. Then, one day, Grossi would come to Hugh and tell him that he needed help with thirty escapees who were hiding outside the city. Grossi had no choice but to go along with the plan.

Hugh naturally agreed to go and see them. Then Grossi mentioned that one of them was sick and would need help getting to Rome ... Concerned, Hugh agreed that of course he would come and say Mass the following week and bring back the sick man to Rome, where he would get him the medical attention he needed. On St Patrick's Day, the day before Hugh was due to go, he was in his rooms, celebrating the feast day with a couple of his helpers, when the phone rang. Hugh picked it up and listened to the voice at the other end. His face grave, he finally said, 'All right, I understand . . . God forgive him.' He had been tipped off – and had forgiven Grossi into the bargain.

Frustrated that Hugh was evading his every attempt to capture him, Kappler decided to get personally involved. First, he decided to do some reconnaissance with a couple of soldiers. They stood behind the white boundary line at St Peter's, and there Hugh was, in his usual place on the steps. Kappler turned to the men and told them that their job was to lure him out over the line. They would attend Mass at St Peter's in a few days' time. On their way out, they would hustle him over the white line and then let him go. Once out in the open, he would be shot.

One of Hugh's helpers, Giuseppe, tipped John May off about the ambush. He knew that the Gestapo would come for Hugh, but was not exactly sure when. John advised Hugh to stay off the steps for a bit. But Hugh wasn't so sure. 'What, me boy, and let them think that I'm afraid? So long as they don't use guns I can tackle any two or three of them with ease, though a scrap would be a bit undignified on the very steps of St Peter's itself, would it not?' he added cheerfully.

More to the point, if he did not appear for a few days and then took up his usual post, the Gestapo might take their chances – and this time he might have no advance warning. John May agreed and decided that the time was ripe to teach Kappler a lesson. As Giuseppe had predicted, the two Germans appeared at Mass a few days later. They lurked in the church, pretending to mingle with the congregation. But Giuseppe was on hand to point them out and before they could move, four Swiss Guards and John May were standing beside them. The game was up.

The German agents prepared to be escorted off Vatican territory and back into Rome. But instead, they were bustled into a side street where they were greeted with a crowd of Yugoslav freedom fighters. These men hated the Germans and were ready to teach them a lesson. The next morning, two very battered and bruised men reported to Kappler.

Hugh had had a lucky escape, but Brother Robert 'Whitebrows' Pace was not so lucky. With two Italian friends he had been visiting POWs in hiding in the countryside when he was arrested by members of Pietro Koch's gang. The POWs were taken to a camp, but Koch had other plans for Brother Robert. Perhaps under torture the Brother would reveal some information about Hugh, he thought.

But Brother Robert was cleverer than that. He told the Fascists that if they cared to check, they would discover that he was known to high-ranking German officers. The Fascists were immediately nervous, scared of upsetting their German masters. And when they checked Brother Robert's story, they discovered that he had been telling the truth. He had nursed German soldiers in his Order's hospital with as much care as the other patients, and the Germans had not forgotten. Pietro Koch was ordered to release him.

But Brother Robert did not return to the hospital. Hugh arranged for him to disappear. He was not seen again until the Americans liberated Rome. His Italian friends were not so lucky. A week later, they were executed.

14 Endgame

It was spring 1944, and the situation in Rome was at an all-time low. The Allies had become stuck in Monte Cassino and liberation looked a very long way away. Rations were reduced to almost nothing, and only those who could afford to pay the high black-market prices could eat properly.

Mother Mary St Luke managed to keep her sense of humour, even at this time. 'Our cat ate a rat,' she noted with great amusement in her diary of 9 May. 'His whole being rose up against a diet of macaroni, dried peas and rice cooked in water with no cheese, no butter, no gravy, no milk.' And so he slunk off to the cellar where he killed and ate an entire rat, 'all except the tail, which we think he is going to appeal to the cook to make into soup for him,' she said dryly. But there is no doubting that conditions were grim. The German authorities were engaged in an increasingly vicious battle with partisans – Italians who wanted to overthrow them. And the battle was about to become deadly.

The Germans had brought in an extra 500 soldiers to control the city. Of these, the Eleventh Company were trainee soldiers, 150 in all, who would march through the city every day at 2 p.m. – a fact which was noticed by the partisans. They watched the troop march round the corner on to Via Rasella, a narrow street lined with tall buildings, which climbs steeply up to the Quirinal Hill. Perfect for an ambush.

The partisans picked the 23 March as the day when they would strike. The authorities had decided that it was a 'celebration day', the twenty-fifth anniversary of Mussolini's founding of the Fascist Party. A number of outdoor events were planned and many German soldiers would be out on the streets, where the partisans would be waiting.

At 2 p.m. a group of men waited on Via Rasella for the marching German soldiers. Nothing. At 3 p.m., there was still no sign. The partisans were about to abort the mission, when, at 3.45 p.m., the column of soldiers marched around the corner, straight into the trap. The explosion of TNT, hidden in a rubbish cart, followed by mortar fire, killed twenty-four soldiers and left thirty others dying or wounded on the streets. Two ordinary Romans were also killed. The partisans vanished into thin air.

At first, the Germans panicked, as one observer noted. 'Everyone was shouting, everyone giving orders. Germans and Fascists kept bursting into dwellings and dragging out men to the desperate cries of women and children . . .' One German general was even seen weeping and 'running around furiously like a mortally stricken beast'.

But once word reached Hitler of the atrocity, German revenge was swift. For every German, ten Italians were to be shot, he ordered. Within twenty-four hours, 335 Italians had been rounded up: partisans, prisoners at Regina Coeli jail, some innocent people who had been arrested on Via Rasella, 75 Jews, anyone even suspected of being anti-Fascist. All of them would be executed. They were taken to the Ardeatine caves, the large tunnels of a disused quarry, and shot. Explosions were then set off in the cave to block off the entrances. The Germans had carried out their killing brutally and in cold blood.

Hugh was in despair. Five of his friends and helpers were among the dead. He might even have been too, had he been captured. He was horrified at the German action and refused to visit the caves until 1947, when the Americans were investigating the crimes that had taken place there. His companion that day, singer Veronica Dunne, recalled his tears during his visit as he knelt on the floor and said a decade of the Rosary for those who had lost their lives.

Because of the German actions, more and more ordinary people wanted to help Hugh: the Italian boy who had tipped them off about the raids on Via Chelini proved to be a real asset. Somehow, he had got hold of papers issued to Germans and Fascists with details of places to be raided.

But at the same time, there were still those who were willing, or could be persuaded, to betray Hugh. They had long suspected that someone was leaking information, and they were right. Perfetti, one of the organisation's oldest recruits, had been arrested. When tortured by Koch, he had cracked and given them the addresses of many of the billets.

Perfetti's arrest would put many of Hugh's key helpers in danger. John Furman was staying with Romeo Giuliani and his wife and family. Gino, his son, was a great help to John, and tipped him off that he knew Perfetti. Sensing danger, John left the apartment and was not there when the Fascists arrived. Under torture, poor Gino cracked, too, and gave them information about many of the hidden places, a disaster for the organisation.

Bill Simpson had not yet heard about Gino when he visited a block of flats just a hundred yards from St Peter's Square. The porter, Paolino, was a staunch friend of the organisation. 'A sprightly, tiny man, perhaps four feet six inches in height. His heart, however, was as big as his stature was small.' Although his own flat was tiny, Paolino sheltered sometimes as many as seven escapees at a time. Bill rang on Paolino's doorbell, but the flat was empty. The tiny man had been dragged away by the Fascists. But first, he had managed to shove five POWs in the cellar and move his bed over the trapdoor entrance. Simpson opened the door to find five pairs of eyes looking at him.

Only a few days later, on 18 April, however, Bill was arrested with an American lieutenant, Dukate, and put into the back of a Gestapo car. Somehow, although a Gestapo officer was sitting on top of him, Bill managed to get rid of any dangerous documents by shoving them out of a window, hoping that whoever found them would not be honest enough to hand them in to the nearest police station. Bill and Dukate were taken to Regina Coeli prison.

15 Fight to the Death

Sam and Hugh were fighting for the survival of the organisation. Between March and May 1944 forty-six of their charges were re-arrested or shot. The Swiss Legation, which had been such a great help to Hugh, was forbidden by the Germans from offering further help and Fathers Borg, Madden and Buckley were ordered to stay in their homes. Hugh was told to stay in the Vatican on fear of death. The situation became more deadly by the day as Pietro Koch's gang became more active.

Sam Derry was forced to take action. He knew that the Fascists were trying harder than ever to capture POWs and that finding safe places for them to stay was more difficult than ever. He also knew that the longer escapees were cooped up indoors, the more likely they were to do something foolish and risk capture. His instructions were firm: no POWs were to be hidden in Rome from then on. POWs were to stay in their homes at all times unless a raid was imminent. And if they had to make a run for it, they must head for the country rather than risk other prisoners by heading for their apartments.

As the Allies drew closer to Rome, the Germans were beginning to panic, cordoning off streets and demanding to see the identity cards of all those caught in their net. Italians who should have been fighting in the War were sent to labour camps in Germany and POWs went straight to prison.

Lieutenant Garrad-Cole was sitting on a tram one day when he noticed two German soldiers looking at him with great interest. He got off the tram at the next stop. The Germans followed. He walked on briskly, then pretended to stop and look into a shop window. The soldiers passed on without even glancing in his direction. 'I sighed with relief and realised for the first time I was bathed in perspiration. But then they stopped about twenty yards away to look in another shop window. My heart sank. Obviously, the Huns were playing me at my own game.'

When the soldiers caught up with him, they demanded to see his identity card. He produced the forged one supplied to him by Hugh's organisation, but the two men were not convinced. They began to escort him down the street. Garrad-Cole glanced at the soldiers, weighing up his chances. They didn't look too big, and their guns where holstered at their waists. Without warning, he stuck his right foot out and tripped up one of the guards, who sprawled on the ground. Garrad-Cole made a run for it, rushing down a nearby street. A moment later, a bullet whined past his shoulder.

Garrad-Cole knew that he had to get off the street. He thought quickly. Renzo Lucidi's flat was around the corner, so he ran in that direction. He hid behind the front entrance as the two soldiers dashed past. Not daring to take to the street again, Garrad-Cole called at Renzo's flat. He had to find a hiding place, and quickly, before the soldiers returned. Renzo had an idea. The lift was called up to the top of the building. 'I climbed on the top of the cage to lie full length in the small space between the top of the cage and the winding gear,' he recalled.

The Germans came back. They combed the apartment block for an hour and found no trace of Garrad-Cole. When they left, Renzo helped Garrad-Cole out of the lift, and into a new disguise, replacing his light-coloured raincoat and black trilby with a dark brown coat and hat. He left the building, accompanied by Renzo's young son Maurice. 'Father' and son received nothing more than a passing glance from German soldiers. Maurice took Garrad-Cole as far as the River Tiber and then left him with a cheery wave to run back home through the streets.

With Bill Simpson in Regina Coeli, John Furman became the Gestapo's next target. He dyed his hair black and shaved off his moustache to make himself look more like an Italian, but even so, a friend warned him that he was next on the Gestapo's Most Wanted list. It fell to Renzo and Adrienne Lucidi to deliver money and supplies to the escapees, 164 in Rome and more than 3,000 in the countryside. Each day they set off, trying to escape the minor explosions and assassinations as the fight between the Germans and the partisans became more bitter.

Giovanni Cecarelli was looking after five men who had been hurriedly moved from Henrietta's flat. He was at home one evening with the five men when there was a loud knock on the door. Heart hammering in his chest, Giovanni shoved the men out on to his tiny living-room balcony and drew the curtains. He answered the door and the Gestapo poured in. They hunted high and low in the tiny flat, finding nothing. Just as they were about to leave, the sergeant pointed to the curtained window. What was through there, he demanded?

'Only the balcony,' Giovanni said, racking his brains to see how he might distract the man. Would he like a drink?

No thanks, he was told, and to his horror, the sergeant went over to the window and pulled back the curtains. Giovanni held his breath, ready for the men to be dragged into the room, and for his fate to be sealed.

Instead, the sergeant came back. 'Balcony's empty,' he announced. And he'd have that drink now, thanks.

Giovanni was astonished. How on earth had the men managed to escape? He managed to serve the drink and when the Gestapo had left, went to investigate. Of course, he stored a ladder on the balcony. The men had used it to climb up to the apartment above and had pulled the ladder up with them.

It was a constant game of cat-and-mouse with the Gestapo and the Fascists, and so many people like Giovanni risked their lives to help others. But there were small signs that things were changing in the city. German women in Rome were ordered to leave the city and there were rumours that the Gestapo would be next. The Romans were growing desperate, as Mother Mary St Luke reported: 'Every day we expect the invasion. Every day we listen to victory talk on the wireless . . . when will they come?' she asked.

As April dragged into May, and the food shortages grew, it seemed that the answer was, 'not soon enough'.

16 Liberation at Last?

As the spring wore on, Hugh was summoned to a meeting with the Holy Father himself. The German Embassy had complained to the Vatican about Hugh's activities, and the Pope gently asked him to stay inside the Vatican for a while and not to attempt to help any POWs. This does not mean that the Pope disapproved of what Hugh was doing – he could easily have asked him to stop on many occasions before – but perhaps he thought Hugh should run no further risks, with the Allies so close and the Germans increasingly reckless. Certainly, Hugh's friend Sam thought so.

But Hugh, being Hugh, still had to help people, even though he could see no one directly. John May had a plan. Those who needed to see Hugh could arrive in the guard room at the Vatican's Santa Marta gate. A call would be made to John, who would appear. He would then pass on messages to Hugh and transmit the answers. That way Hugh could continue to do his work without risking his life.

But just as it seemed the situation could continue for ever, the Allies made progress south of the city and liberation looked suddenly not so far away. Mother Mary St Luke noted that 'the offensive on the Via Rasella has put new life into us, and new hope into the Italians. The Allies are progressing slowly, but as long as they do progress, all is well.'

And they did progress. Each night, the sound of gunfire could be heard in the hills around the city. At the same time, the Germans were preparing to leave. They had packed their belongings and waited for the signal. It was rumoured that they would abandon the city as soon as the Allies attempted a landing – maybe as soon as 22 May. Some Romans were overjoyed at this news, but others were more cautious, dreading what the Germans might do to the city before they left.

Knowing that the situation was tense, Sam Derry reminded all POWs of their orders to say put and not to wander the streets. But one day, two of them decided to disobey: knowing that a good meal would be provided by Henrietta Chevalier, they called into her tiny flat. They did not realise that Henrietta's flat was now being watched at all times by two SS officers posted on the street. They had already grilled the porter, Edigio, and were waiting for the little Maltese woman to make a false move.

The two young men knocked on her door and when

she opened it and saw them, she was horrified. She shooed them away – 'the Germans are watching!' – and closed the door firmly. The only way out was down the stairs and through the front door, which the two did as quickly as possible. But as they slipped onto the street, a man sitting in a café opposite them got up and followed them. The two young men made a run for it, losing themselves in the narrow streets, before vanishing into thin air.

Sam heard nothing from them for days, until they suddenly reappeared at another flat, but once Hugh heard about the danger in which Henrietta had been placed, he decided that she and her family needed to get away. And so, one at a time, each member of the family left the flat – but never returned. They left with no baggage, so that the SS would not be suspicious, and made their way separately into the countryside, where they stayed until the Germans left the city.

John Furman was in awe of Henrietta's bravery: 'I would not call her brave for it seemed to me that she had no conception of fear. Her kindness and generosity were unparalleled, her maternal spirit and compassion boundless,' he said admiringly. It was only fitting that Hugh would see to it that she could be safe with her family.

With German defeat only three weeks away, the military seemed anxious to do as much damage as it could before leaving the city. On 1 May Hugh was devastated to find that his great friend Anselmo

Musters, code-named 'Dutchpa', had been arrested. He had just left a billet when he became aware that he was being followed. Every time he stopped, his follower stopped, too, and pretended to look in a shop window. Fr Musters strolled on but changed direction and made for the safety of the Basilica of Santa Maria Maggiore.

Before he got there, the man caught up with him. 'Your papers,' he demanded.

Father Anselmo tried to make a run for it into the church, but the man jumped in front of him and pulled a pistol from inside his coat. 'Stop,' he ordered. When Father Musters struggled, the man hit him a vicious blow on the head.

A Palatine Guard, seeing the commotion, dragged Anselmo inside the church and called for help. The Vatican told the guard and Father Anselmo to stay where they were. They would be safe inside the church, in Vatican territory. They were wrong. About half an hour later, the church was surrounded and the Gestapo marched in. Father Anselmo was ordered to follow them and when he refused, he was hit again by a sub-machine gun, dragged down the steps and taken to Gestapo headquarters.

The Germans were delighted, thinking that they had captured a British colonel in disguise. They stripped Father Anselmo, removing his shoes, handcuffing his hands and manacling his feet. Every day for a fortnight, in the prison on Via Tasso, Father Anselmo was interrogated by the Gestapo. The two officers, Schulz and Wolf, were relentless. What did he know about Hugh's organisation? How did it help POWs?

Father Anselmo refused to reveal anything. They even showed him a diagram of the organisation and its activities, which Anselmo was horrified to see was very accurate. Again, he said nothing. Finally, after two weeks, they threw him in prison, and then onto the notorious train bound for Germany. Like Furman and Pollak before him, Anselmo knew that his only choice was to jump. At Florence, he escaped and made his way back to Rome.

The arrest of Father Anselmo was one of the Gestapo's last acts in Rome because, within days, the Allies were within striking range of the city. They had taken Monte Cassino on 18 May, after four hard months, during which 100,000 Allied soldiers were killed or injured and that city destroyed. 'Explosions and the sound of artillery reaches us fitfully by night and by day at present,' noted Mother Mary St Luke, seeing a steady stream of refugees who had escaped from prison camps pass her window.

But there was still no immediate sign of liberation. Even though the Gestapo had all but disappeared, the Romans were afraid that the enemy might try to take their prisoners with them out of Rome to concentration camps, or even to shoot them on the spot. The last days of the Germans in Rome were still deadly.

17 Freedom

Adrienne Lucidi had a plan. It involved their old friend, the suspected double agent Cipolla. With the end of the war in sight, he was keen to make friends with the Allies and Adrienne thought it was time he had his chance. He would tell the Germans that he had made contact with Hugh's organisation and that he could gain access to it. In return, the Germans would release two prisoners, Bill Simpson and John Armstrong.

The Germans were interested. Cipolla was shown a list of all prisoners at Regina Coeli prison – but neither name was on it. Where could they be? Just then, Bill Simpson managed to smuggle information out of the prison: he was using a false identity, that of William O'Flynn. Hugh despaired – how could he help Bill without revealing him to be a British spy and not an innocent Irishman? He would certainly be executed.

As so often happened for Hugh, fate intervened. One day, he received word that a Roman gentleman wished to see him. They chatted for a while about a mutual friend, whilst Hugh wondered about the real purpose of the man's visit. He was astonished when the man revealed that he had come to seek Hugh's help – on behalf of Pietro Koch. He could hardly believe it, until the man revealed the bargain. If Hugh would help Koch's wife and mother, Koch would see to it that all prisoners in Regina Coeli prison would be left alone when the Allies marched in – and not transported to their deaths in Germany.

Hugh saw his chance. He would help Koch's family, but only if Koch would guarantee the release of Simpson and Armstrong.

The next day, Bill and his friend were in their cell when a voice called out 'Bill Simpson. John Armstrong.' Was it a trap? Neither dared respond. The gentleman returned to visit Hugh. No one had answered to that name in the prison. Hugh was frustrated, but asked the man to tell Koch to look for William O'Flynn. As far as he knew 'Armstrong' was his friend's real name. But he had run out of time. The Allies surrounded Rome and the Germans got ready to leave.

Many Romans held their breath, waiting to see what the retreating Germans would do. In the middle of the night of 1 June, the German Ambassador, Von Weizsaecker, was called to the Vatican to see the Pope. Mother Mary St Luke noted in her diary that night that, 'A fresh rumour . . . says insistently that the Pope has promised the Germans that if they do no damage to the city as they withdraw, he will make himself responsible for all their wounded . . .'

Hitler had sent orders to Field Marshal Kesselring on 3 June to defend the city at all costs, if necessary to blow up the bridges across the Tiber. But Kesselring had clearly decided otherwise. As the Allies poured into the area around Rome, 'like water through a dyke', according to Mother Mary St Luke, the Germans packed into lorries to leave the city.

But Hugh could not rest easy. There were 400 Russians hidden by his organisation in the city. They needed special care, as the Germans regarded them as bitter enemies and might try to execute them on their way out of the city. Hugh organised for the Russians to be sent to new homes, explaining to Sam: 'Have you got any cash about, me boy? I have a wee problem. We want to shift some Russians to make sure these Germans don't get 'em, but the landladies want their money first!'

Sam Derry produced a wad of cash and joked, 'I hope Joe Stalin pays it back.'

For Bill Simpson in Regina Coeli prison, liberation could not come soon enough. It was 30 May, and the prisoners could hear distant gunfire. And then a new group of prison guards appeared – Austrians. The Germans had vanished overnight. Within two days, the doors of the prison were thrown open and Bill and his friends simply walked out to freedom.

John Furman was trying to concentrate on the organisation's accounts with Renzo Lucidi, in spite of the fact that all around him was chaos. They were sitting in Renzo's flat when the doorbell rang – it was the secret ring which only those of the organisation knew. 'Could this be a trap?' he wondered. 'A last-minute effort by the Gestapo or Koch's gang? We waited tensely while Peppina [the housemaid] opened the door. We heard a scream,' he reported. It was none other than Bill Simpson, returned at last.

But John Armstrong was not so lucky. The Germans had taken fourteen prisoners with them on their retreat from Regina Coeli. On their way out of the city, they had a change of heart. It would simply be too much trouble to take these men all the way to Germany with them. And so on 4 June, as the Allies marched into the city, the fourteen men were executed. It is fairly certain that one of these men was Armstrong. But there was a final twist: he wasn't 'Armstrong' at all, but a secret agent, code-named Gabriel.

As the Germans left, the Romans looked on, but did not retaliate. 'The boot was on the other leg, the wheel had gone full circle and the defeated Huns were escaping in disorder . . . the Germans went on, wild-eyed, unshaven, unkempt, on foot, in stolen cars, in horse-drawn vehicles . . . they were frightened,' Mother Mary St Luke noted in her diary.

A Swiss journalist, M. de Wyss, looked at the

retreating Germans, 'their faces grey with fatigue, eyes popping out, mouths wide open, they limped barefoot, dragging their rifles after them. I remember the same army entering France, contemptuous, almighty, trampling over the weaker. I remembered being thrown into a ditch by them. Now I was witnessing their defeat. My jaws clenched.' She was reflecting the emotions of many Italians who had suffered under the German regime.

And then came the celebrations. The Allies had entered Rome. People filled the streets. The electricity, which had been shut off, was restarted. The whole city came to life. Mother Mary St Luke opened her window at dawn on 5 June to see a lone American jeep, with four American soldiers in it, making its way along the street. 'The thing looked so solitary and yet so significant in the cool stillness of dawn . . . a full stop at the end of the chapter of oppression and fear.'

Harold Tittman, the US Representative, was in the convent garden when a convoy of American jeeps passed, driving north after the Germans. The jeep stopped as the Tittman family shouted hello in English. 'Obviously surprised, one of the soldiers asked us who we were. When he learned that we were Americans, he reached to the back of the vehicle, pulled out a carton of cigarettes, a box of Hershey bars and a copy of *Time* magazine. This was our first, happy contact with American soldiers.'

Monsignor O'Flaherty meets General Mark Clark, who led the liberating troops into Rome.

The people of Rome were elated – happy that their city was theirs once more. More importantly, the Allies brought into the city much needed food supplies. The locals had been existing on very meagre rations and the food was more than welcome. But for others, the end of the conflict in Rome brought mixed feelings. The sense of purpose which had carried them through was no longer there. And now some were not really sure what to do.

John Furman was out and about on this historic day in June. He approached the driver of a jeep to shake his hand.

'Say, you speak good English for an *Italiano*,' the soldier remarked.

'That's perhaps because I'm English,' he replied with a smile.

'Well, whaddya know? Say, what are you doing here anyway?'

Suddenly, John thought of his wife at home and his two-year-old daughter, whom he had never seen. He wondered what he *was* doing in this city any more. 'Just playing hide-and-seek,' he joked to the puzzled American.

Perhaps now, he thought, it was really time to go home.

18 New Beginnings

For Hugh O'Flaherty, the end of the War in Rome meant many things. He was proclaimed a hero by many, receiving a number of awards for bravery. To others, he was an attention-seeker, even a spy for the British. Many were jealous of his high position in the Vatican. But what is sure is that he attacked life after the War with the same energy and sense of purpose. He also showed true Christian kindness to those who had once been his enemy.

The ending of the occupation of Rome brought new diplomatic tensions to the Vatican. The Lateran Treaty, signed by Benito Mussolini in 1929, had made the Vatican an independent city-state and the Germans had respected this all through the War. This meant that the ambassadors of 'enemy' countries, like Britain and America, were allowed to stay in the Vatican. Ironically, the British ignored this treaty and ordered its diplomats to leave. At this moment, the German Ambassador, Von

Weizsaecker, moved into the Vatican. It was a very lucky move. The war in Europe was far from over, and on 20 July, there was an attempt to assassinate Adolf Hitler. One of the chief suspects was Von Weizsaecker. He had always been anti-Nazi, and it seemed fitting that the Vatican had saved him.

For the British, the end of the occupation of Rome meant a new task: helping British and other POWs to go home. Sam Derry found himself a new role as head of a 'repatriation' unit, helping the escapees to rejoin their army units, or to find their way home. He was helped by Bill Simpson and John Furman, among others.

One of his first jobs was to repay all of the money borrowed on behalf of Hugh's organisation during the War. The records of the organisation had been buried in biscuit tins in the Vatican gardens, and were now dug up. Derry had kept careful records and was able to repay as much as £1 million pounds in cash to those who had helped.

Typically, Hugh now turned his attention to the German prisoners of war. He asked the American Commander, Mark Clark, to assure him that they were being well treated. He also helped Austrians who had fought for the Germans. When asked why, his answer was simple: 'God has no country.'

One of the first people Hugh visited was his old enemy, Kappler. The former Gestapo man, called 'the executioner of Rome' because of his actions during the War, was in prison near Naples. The German had been responsible for the brutal killings at the Ardeatine Caves, and for sending more than 10,000 Italian Jews to their deaths in concentration camps. But every month, Kappler had a visitor from Rome: Hugh O'Flaherty.

Many were horrified at Hugh's actions. 'He has become Kappler's number one protector,' cried the newspaper, *Avanti*, even suggesting that Hugh might be trying to get Kappler freed. But of course, this was not the case. Hugh was simply doing his duty as a priest: to show Christian compassion to those in need, regardless of what they had done. To Hugh, everyone, even Herbert Kappler, was worthy of God's love. When Kappler became a Roman Catholic some years later, Hugh was there to baptise him.

One young Irishman whom Hugh helped was Billy Vincent, a captain in the Inniskilling Fusiliers, whose family came from Killarney. Wounded in battle, Billy was sent to hospital in Rome, where Hugh took him under his wing. When Billy recovered, he wanted to thank Hugh and asked him if there was anything he needed.

'I would like a pair of army boots like you have, if you could get them,' was the reply.

Surprised, Billy asked Hugh why. 'He lifted up his foot and there were hardly any soles on his shoes. He had been walking all over Rome during the War with really only the uppers of his shoes. I was amazed. I would never have thought he had suffered in this way.'

But Billy did not know Hugh O'Flaherty well. The priest never thought of himself. He saw it as his duty to put others first and would not have given a thought to his own comfort. Even on the day Rome was liberated, Hugh told Sam. '"Well, my lad, there is work to be done," and off he went into the city to visit some of our helpers and their relations who had suffered so much .. . on our behalf,' Sam reported.

When the Supreme Allied Commander in Italy, General Harold Alexander, came to visit Hugh to thank him, Hugh's only interest was how the Allies were going to help the Italian families who had suffered. Many Italian prisoners of war had been captured in North Africa, then Italian territory, and transported to prison in South Africa, thousands of miles from home. With Alexander's help, Hugh was able to travel there and make sure that all were well and able to communicate with their families while waiting to go home. He also flew to Israel when the state was established, to see if homes could be found here for the many Jews whom he had helped during the War.

Hugh didn't see the difference between enemy and friend and when Dr Cipolla was tried as a traitor, of course he testified on his behalf. 'They did wrong, but there is good in every man,' he explained to the astonished Sam Derry.

New Beginnings

Hugh's heroic work earned him many honours after the War. He was awarded the CBE – Commander of the British Empire – by the British (along with many other priests including Fathers Borg, Madden and Buckley and the brave Henrietta Chevalier). Even so, being listed in the paper as a 'British resident in Rome' would no doubt have annoyed him. Hugh was a proud Irishman, who loved his country.

The Americans recognised him too, awarding him the Silver Palm for his outstanding services to the government of the United States. 'His untiring energy and efforts, often at the risk of his own life, and his unfailing devotion to the cause of freedom were exemplified in the concrete aid given to so many prisoners of war,' it was declared.

With the end of the War, Hugh could play his beloved golf once more, though typically, he used this as an opportunity to help people. When playing golf at a course near Ciampino, he noticed how poor the local people were, and decided to take up their cause personally. For the next twelve years, he saw to it that they received good food from Rome and regularly said Mass in the tiny, half-ruined church there. Many of his friends sent clothes parcels from the best stores in New York and London, so the locals were very well dressed!

But life after the War also had its difficulties for Hugh. Once, in 1946, he was at home in Ireland and visited a priest in County Kildare, where a beautiful meal was served. But he was hardly able to touch it. The food was simply too rich after his poor diet in Rome. He also had to suffer the jealousies of others. There were many in the Vatican who felt that only Italians should work there and Hugh sometimes found the politics there too much. More significantly, there were whispers that Hugh had been a British spy during the War.

Some, even in Irish diplomatic circles, criticised Hugh. They felt he had boasted of the money given to him by wealthy Romans to help the escapees and that in return for his help with POWs, he had been rewarded by trips to South Africa. Some even went so far as to think him an agent for the British government.

It is hard to know just why these people were suspicious of Hugh. Perhaps they were worried for other Irish citizens living in Rome had Hugh been captured. But Hugh helped not just British soldiers in finding shelter and providing identity cards: he helped *everyone*, ally and enemy alike.

Monsignor Hugh O'Flaherty.

19 A Gentle Giant

Who was Hugh O'Flaherty? He never kept a diary or recorded any of his exploits, so his innermost thoughts remain hidden. To Hugh, the work was everything, doing, rather than recording. But he made an impact on everyone he met and their memories of this man are vivid.

The historian Raleigh Travelyan remembers 'A magnetic character, fanatically keen on golf, tall, a considerable joker, with a thick brogue and blue eyes behind round steel-rimmed spectacles.' It was Travelyan who first referred to Hugh as 'a scarlet pimpernel', a man who used every resource to help others, and who skilfully evaded capture.

John Furman remembered him as, 'A very good friend who made other people's troubles his own.' Sam Derry remembered 'his courage, his faith in God and people, his kindness, his devotion and his indifference to personal comfort . . .' He described Hugh's determination to do what needed to be done and quickly, and his untiring work ethic. 'However tired we might be after walking the many many miles around Rome visiting and transporting chaps to billets, we would return to his bed study which we shared and he . . . would work at his desk until the early hours.' Sam recalled that his strongest ability was 'to see the best in people, even the vilest creatures who were capable of terrible deeds, he would feel that there must be some good in them somewhere.'

To help those who needed it, Hugh risked his own life and engaged the loyalty of many other volunteers. This group of people came from all walks of life, from priests to porters, nurses to butchers, from princes and princesses to those who had almost nothing. What is clear is that Hugh inspired in them great courage and resourcefulness. Inspired by his example, they sheltered POWs and other escapees, knowing that if they were caught, imprisonment was certain. They hid them with great ingenuity, knowing what needed to be done should the Gestapo appear. None of this would have been possible without the great leadership of Hugh O'Flaherty. Sam Derry was convinced. 'Had it not been for this gallant gentleman, there would have been no Rome Escape Organisation.'

Many people have wondered why Hugh is not recognised more for the work he did. Partly, this is because some disapproved of it, not that this would have upset him unduly, but also because it was not in Hugh's

From left to right: Hugh O'Flaherty, Sam Derry and presenter Eamonn Andrews, after the BBC's This is Your Life *programme on 19 February 1963.*

nature to seek attention. He was simply doing what needed to be done and no more.

But in 1962, the producers of a popular TV programme, *This is Your Life*, took a great interest in the work of Hugh O'Flaherty. They decided to devote a programme to his life. Sadly, Hugh was too ill to travel to London and so Sam Derry became the focus of the show. Old friends, including Bill Simpson and John Furman gathered in the TV studio to pay tribute to the organisation. Norman Anderson came on to talk about the operation on his appendix which had saved his life. As the programme drew to a close the presenter, Irishman Eamonn Andrews, announced that they had time for one more guest.

'Suddenly Monsignor appeared and slowly walked on stage. Blinking in the limelight, he grinned and threw his arms around me. We both wept for joy. That was our last time together,' Sam recalled.

The audience was filled with those who had been helped by Hugh's organisation, many of whom had never even met the Monsignor. Now, at last, they had the chance to thank him in person. And even though he was by now very ill, Hugh had travelled to London to be reunited with his old friends one last time.

Hugh died on 30 October 1963, having suffered a stroke. He is buried in Cahersiveen. He was remembered by his old friend Father Francis Joy as 'a generous, honest-to-God Irishman without guile. His big heart was open to any and every distress . . . his life was always ordered to using his powers . . . for the Glory of God. Can any of us hope to achieve more?'

A grove of Italian trees in Killarney National Park, County Kerry, commemorates this extraordinary Irishman and a road in Killarney was named after him in 2008.